JEWISH ART

ITS HISTORY FROM THE BEGINING
TO THE PRESENT DAY

JEWISH ART

ITS HISTORY FROM THE BEGINING
TO THE PRESENT DAY

ERNST COHN-WIENER

Afterword by
HANNELORE KÜNZL

Translation by
ANTHEA BELL

PILKINGTON PRESS

Dedication
From the publisher to his wife Esther
in joyful celebration of their silver wedding anniversary
23 December 2000

FIRST PUBLISHED BERLIN, 1929
NEW GERMAN EDITION:
GEBR. MANN VERLAG, BERLIN 1995

PUBLISHED IN ENGLISH TRANSLATION 2001
BY PILKINGTON PRESS LTD
YELVERTOFT MANOR
NORTHAMPTONSHIRE NN6 6LF

ISBN 1 899044 27 2

PRODUCED, DESIGNED AND TYPESET BY:
A.H. JOLLY (EDITORIAL) LTD
YELVERTOFT MANOR
NOTHAMPONSHIRE NN6 6LF

PRINTED IN GREAT BRITAIN

CONTENTS

INTRODUCTION
The Basic Question
Page 7

Israel and its art – The religious foundations – The artistic foundations –
Dependency on the art of other nations – Predominance of the spiritual element

CHAPTER 1
THE LAND THAT ISRAEL CONQUERED
Page 17

The nomadic period of Israel – The tabernacle – The culture of Canaan before the
Israelite conquest – Religious monuments – Fortifications – Houses –
Egyptian influence – Ceramics – The art of the Philistines

CHAPTER 2
THE TIME OF THE KINGS
Page 34

Historical development – David's buildings – Solomon's buildings – Their
furnishings – Israel and Phoenicia – The art of the later period of the Kings –
Seals – Ceramics

CHAPTER 3
ISRAEL AMONG THE PEOPLES OF ANTIQUITY
Page 63

The cultural atmosphere – The second temple – Hellenism and the art of the
Maccabean period – The fortress of Arak el Emir – Herod's temple –
Its equipment – Herod's buildings in Samaria – Gerasa – The synagogues of
Palestine – Their symbolism – Tombs and tomb paintings – Egypt – Malta –
Sicily – Jewish painting – Synagogues of the eastern Mediterranean –
North Africa – Rome – The catacombs – Sarcophagi – Gold glasses

CHAPTER 4

GOLUSS (EXILE) AND GHETTO

Page 134

Jewish artists in the ghetto – Islam – Spanish synagogues – Jewish manuscripts
of the Islamic period – The Gothic influence – Illuminated manuscripts –
Jewish art in Italy – Furniture – Synagogues and their equipment –
More illuminated manuscripts – Printed books – Sephardi art in Holland –
England – Poland – Wooden synagogues – Jewish cultic utensils

CHAPTER 5

THE WAY TO THE PRESENT DAY

Page 227

The 18th century – The first painters – Bendemann and Oppenheim – Jewish
architects – Erich Mendelsohn – Jewish craftsmanship – Painting – Israels –
Pissarro – Max Liebermann – Jewish impressionists – Lesser Ury –
The first consciously Jewish artists – Jewish expressionists –
The future of Jewish art

AFTERWORD
To the 1929 Edition
Page 262

AFTERWORD
To the 1995 Edition
Page 264

TRANSLATOR'S NOTE

The abbreviations BCE (Before Common, or Christian, Era) and CE (Common, or
Christian, Era) have been used in dates. They correspond precisely to BC and AD.

INTRODUCTION

The Basic Question

IS THERE such a thing as Jewish art? The usual answer is no. It is not discussed in mainstream art history or in the reference books. In Jewry itself, although whole libraries of books have been written about the history of the Jews, their literature, their religious and devotional history, art history of any significant extent refers only to Jewish artists of today, whose work is very often not noticeably Jewish. Proud as the Jews have every right to be of their intellectual attainments, they regard their artistic achievements with suspicion and tend to say little about them. Although there is no shortage of Jewish scholars, almost everything written about the Jewish art of the past is by non-Jews. We obviously value our religious and intellectual past far more highly than its artistic equivalent, and feel that Jewish art in itself is not a legitimate concept, or at best is merely to be tolerated.

Indeed there never could have been any Jewish art, as such, of the range and significance of Egyptian or Greek art. The pictorial representation of holy beings – gods, sacred creatures, heroes – was at the very heart of those cultures. The intensity of religious feeling nurtured the imagination and created the art. Israel itself, as the older strata of the Bible make clear, once lived on a cultural level when people imagined their God acting like a human being, although a human being with enormously enhanced powers. It is extraordinarily difficult for nations, or indeed individuals, to shake off the impressions conveyed by their immediate environment and come to believe in something transcendental, not bound to the structures of the visible world. Israel, however, took this step of intellectual liberation remarkably early and followed it through

FIG. 1 S. Hirszenberg, *Goluss.*
Berlin, art collection of the Jewish community.

with great consistency. It led to the acknowledgement of one God, a
wholly spiritual and immaterial being, whom it was therefore impossible
either to imagine or to depict. A dividing line was drawn between the
world of reality and the mystical world, beyond the scope of experience,
which rules it, and was drawn with a precision arising from Israel's
intellectual clarity and critical need for exactitude.

Here Israel was in complete contrast to most of the other peoples of
antiquity, particularly the Greeks. It is not surprising that the battles of
the Maccabees were so hard fought, for they were a clash between the
two diametrical opposites of antiquity. Hellas was a sensuous nation. The
Greeks had to be able to imagine a god in human terms, even if they
believed that god to be immortal, and in their opinion the world was too
richly diverse for them to be content with a single god. The ultimate
expression of the Hellenic idea of the divine is not the incorporeal,
ineffable god, but the beautiful god who delights the eye. Hellas regarded
Pheidias's statue of Zeus as a religious pinnacle, the culmination of its
religious intensity. Israel detested religious intensity in the depiction of a
god to the point of revulsion.

The Israelite stratum can be immediately distinguished from the

FIG. 2 Max Liebermann, *The Judengasse in Amsterdam*, 1887.

Canaanite stratum in Palestine, the Jewish synagogue from the Greek temple or the mediaeval church, by the categorical absence of pictorial images. None the less, there has always been Jewish art.

The third of the Ten Commandments in fact condemned idolatry, not art. In early times the only reason for creating images was religious anyway: all art was religious art. The Third Commandment and the religious conviction which gave rise to it were strong enough to induce an imaginative asceticism, imposing the avoidance of 'graven' or pictorial images on everything that might have developed into great art in Israel. However, it is unjust and does not go to the root of the problem to see this attitude as mere rejection. It was not in the nature of a protest, like the attitude of the Byzantine iconoclasts and their Dutch counterparts. Instead, the entire nation was fundamentally inclined to take another direction, and it did so, adhering to its principles with a rigidity which entirely isolates it in the ancient world. Its lavish Oriental imagination was diverted from images to words, creating myths and laws, devotional structures, songs and prayers.

All pictorial art has sensuous roots. It implies the capacity to experience ideas in images and make them works of art. The abstract and purely intellectual is alien to it, because an idea can only be thought, not visualized, still less depicted. Expressing it pictorially always implies compromise. Hence the origin of allegory: a symbol artistically mean-ingless in itself, its value lying in the idea behind it. Such a course of artistic development is illustrated particularly clearly in Mesopotamia, a land with fateful associations for Israel. As long the art of Mesopotamia was still in touch with nature, its pictorial images were still narratives and its divinities nature gods – i.e. up to the end of the reign of Assur – it remained imaginative and lively. The Persian religion, however, was Zoroastrianism, the cult of Ahura Mazda, with its clear ethical basis in the abstract opposition of good and evil, light and darkness, and at this period art becomes 'nobler', its structures more idealistic but at the same time lacking in originality. A few types remain, their faces entirely unexpressive. The more abstract the religious concepts, the deeper the meaning of a work of art, the more conventional it must be, because it is bound to interpret rather than create. Logically, pictorial representation should be abandoned entirely and only poetry tolerated, since words can deal satisfactorily with the purely intellectual.

Fig. 3 Lesser Ury, *Moses.*

This was exactly what Israel aimed for. The complete spirituality and intellectual purity of its religious impulses account for its ban on graven images – and this at a cultural stage when the Egyptians were not only creating statues of human beings but literally identifying statue and humanity. Painting and sculpture had thus become impossible in Israel. It was necessary to dispense with them if the Old Testament was to be validated as both doctrine and literature.

There was no Jewish will to create art, then – but there was still Jewish art. That sounds like a paradoxical statement, and yet today, when we know more about the instinctive element in art, it is obvious. Art cannot be either deliberately willed into existence or prohibited. It is present in the nomad's tent and the shepherd's pitcher, and lives in every structure, whatever its purpose. For it would be wrong to take 'art' as meaning only the products of personal creative impulse, the works of Michelangelo and Raphael, Dürer and Rembrandt. Such a view came only with the advent of individualism during what we now call the Renaissance. It accompanied the vanity that signs every picture, even every sketch, with a name not always worth recording. In primitive times mankind made implements for a distinct purpose. Art for no purpose, art for art's sake, was inconceivable. Every work made served some end, and was created to serve it. It was not any uglier for that reason than it would be at a later date, merely plainer and often clearer and more beautiful. Images of gods were made as cult objects or for magical purposes. Often they were not figures, simply fetishes. However, human ambition to make its own mark was never an important factor, only the work itself. Even the Canaanite idols, the little Astartes, primitive clay figures found in large quantities during excavations, were made as amulets, not works of art. This, however, is where Israel drew the line, strictly prohibiting any image of God because it might cloud and obscure the great concept of the divinity. Even the mere imagining of God, the idea that such a thing is possible, detracts slightly from the sublimity of the concept. The Israelite imagination, then, was not sensuous but intellectual and spiritual, and yet like all imagination it was still active in the unconscious and always seeking ways to emerge. When a way did open up, it broke out again and again and became creative, for the absence of pictorial images does not mean an absence of structural form. Consequently, Jewish art existed in all periods, if we understand art in the wider and only valid sense of all constructive creativity. Architecture and works of handicraft were not subject to the prohibition, and they existed in Israel at every period. Divine service and domestic architecture called for buildings and utensils: these functional requirements were always supplied, and kept the artistic

FIG. 4 The so-called Graves of the Kings.

13

imagination busy. The problem arose with the question of ornamentation.

Here there is a surprising difference of perception between the Jewish time of the Kings and all later centuries. One would expect to find the ban on ornamentation most strictly applied during the Biblical period, yet the precise opposite is the case. A decorative style which is nothing short of heathen, involving the figurative depiction of demons and animals, was tolerated in the inmost sanctuary of Solomon's temple. Obviously, the Israel of this period was still culturally close to its heathen environment: images were avoided only in its concept of divinity – a very significant feature at the time, and indeed the very reason for the ban on graven images. Only over the centuries, while Jewish religion as a whole moved further towards the abstract, and particularly after the loss of its concrete central point, the temple in Jerusalem, did the idea of the prohibition become so deeply embedded that all pictorial images in general came to be regarded as heathen. The wish to define the national boundaries of Jewry more distinctly in the spiritual as well as the physical domain, to give external expression to an internal contrast, must have played a part in this intensification. However, not all images were inconceivable. There was always ornamental decoration of buildings and tombs, figures were depicted in works of craftsmanship, there was always illustration in books. Josephus expressed the basic, guiding principle very clearly: no free-standing sculpture and no figurative images in connection with holy things were tolerated in Israel. Reliefs and decorative painting, therefore, were permissible if they were not close to or associated with the Most High. This was a principle that could be interpreted in different ways. The constraints to which art was subject were not very clearly defined, but only very strict teachers of the law demanded an entire absence of ornamentation. Synagogues were nearly always lavishly decorated, and ornamentation came as far as the doors of the ark of the Torah and the ribbons around the scroll. Buildings, manuscripts and utensils always offered the creatively gifted artist scope for achievement. In general, one can say that Judaism was no more narrow-minded than Islam in its attitude to ornamentation, and indeed was more tolerant of figurative art.

Like all art, however, Jewish art was the end product of its own soul.

FIG. 5 The old cemetery of the Jewish community of Worms.

Israel's fate after the loss of its independence was to enjoy freedom and *joie de vivre* only for a few centuries at the most. After that, an ever-deepening sense of oppression set in, engendering fear and mental bondage. The free power of creativity that wrests everything possible from the imagination could never thrive in the ghetto, and its inmates were subject to gloomy brooding. One can trace the narrowing constraints of the creative circle from century to century. Those internal bonds were broken only in the present, when the external fetters fell away.

That fact also explains what distinguishes Jewish art, to its detriment, from the art of all other peoples. In its structural principles and style it is dependent, like the Jewish people themselves. It has no absolute independence. We expect the art of a nation to express its unique character, to have its own style. German, Dutch and Italian art, for instance, are self-contained units differing from each other, even completely contrasting. There is no point in turning a blind eye here, and denying that in *this* sense it is true that Jewish art does not exist.

This book, then, will follow its subject through the history of art as a whole. In every land where the Israelites lived they had artistic requirements for worship and for everyday life, and in all those lands they made do with the forms present in their environment, structures derived from very different faiths and races. That was so in the Biblical time of the Kings, the politically most important and independent period of Jewish history, and it is far more evident during the Diaspora. Israel lived through the styles of late antiquity, Islamic and Byzantine styles, the Gothic, Renaissance and Baroque periods, and built and created in all these styles, just as its modern painters today are impressionists and expressionists. This looks like a constant process of assimilation, a featureless absence of personality making its way through the centuries, and yet it is no such thing, for the attitude of Jewish art is always its own, and specifically Jewish. A Jew is not so much concerned with his own style in his works of art but with his own content, the content of his religion. Form is only the means to him, not an end in itself. The basic idea of the Jewish religion, that man sees what is before his eyes but God sees into the heart, provides the best explanation of why content rather than artistic form interested the Israelites. Consequently, there was never a specifically Jewish style, but Jewish symbols and architectural forms were ever-present. For Judaism, form is only a hieroglyphic denoting the spiritual concept it sets out to express. And in looking at Jewish art, one sometimes feels as if the history of art in general has set too high a value on form as opposed to content.

The survey above defines the limitations of this book, but also its possibilities. Jewish people, like any others, have always found artistic expression for their ideas, and in this sense there is certainly such a thing as Jewish art. It has never attained the profundity achieved by Israel in doctrine and literature, but it accompanies the nation throughout its history. Israel has undoubtedly been a nation of *thinkers* rather than *creators*, with greater literary than artistic gifts. But its use of structural form casts some very interesting light on its soul, even where that soul remains very silent. The deepest things are usually those that turn inwards.

CHAPTER ONE

The Land that Israel Conquered

WHEN ISRAEL took possession of its land, the eastern areas under the leadership of Moses and those west of the Jordan from the time of Joshua onwards, its military might was immense. The conquest went energetically ahead, unbroken by any resistance or setbacks. The fanaticism of the Israelite warriors, who were not just conquering land but fulfilling a religious mission, has no counterpart except perhaps in the conquests of Islam. However, to understand the kind of culture Israel had to create after settling in the land, it is important to know what it found there.

Israel was a nomadic nation, and it was a long time before the people really became sedentary town-dwellers. This cultural change occupied the entire period of the Judges and a large part of the time of the Kings. Deborah is still addressing her people thus: 'Tell of it, you who ride on tawny asses, you who sit on rich carpets and you who walk by the way.' In the field of art, this means that Israel cannot have brought any art of its own to Canaan that required established workshops or made works to last. The people lived in tents that could be struck easily, and their possessions had to be portable. There was no architecture – an art which is bound to the soil – and craftsmanship must have been on a very restricted scale. We may assume that there were fabrics and carpets that could be rolled up and taken with the people as they travelled on, and would be ready for use again at every new camping site. Such textiles have always been the nomad's substitute for furniture and the walls of houses. Again, clay is not really a suitable material for a nomadic tribe's vessels. Shaping clay pots and firing them is a technique that has been known since the distant past of humanity, but they are fragile, the manufacturing process is linked to the presence of a source of clay, and fire on the hearth, and so the vessels of nomadic tribes are usually made of hollowed wood, while their larger containers are woven basketwork. The equipment of the Israelites during their wanderings in the desert and their invasion of Canaan will have been of this kind, and naturally none of it has been preserved.

The question of whether or not Israel had any art before the conquest of Canaan centres on the account of the tabernacle in the desert. As described, it was a work of brilliant imaginative power. No other nomadic tribe could have had anything like it. The ark of the covenant was at the centre of the cult, and was a chest larger than man-size, made of acacia wood overlaid with gold, carried on staves also overlaid with gold and crowned with golden cherubim. The tent of the tabernacle itself consisted of ten enormous 'curtains of fine twined linen, and blue, and purple, and scarlet', protected by a covering of animal skins on the outside. These textiles surrounded the actual tabernacle, which was made of wooden boards. The greatest expenditure of materials and labour went on the ritual objects: the table for the showbread, the seven-branched candlestick, the altar and its appurtenances. Even the court around the tabernacle in the camp was closed off with hangings borne on silver staves between copper poles.

The complexity of the tabernacle, the careful planning of its design and layout, and the magnificence and abundance of its equipment all assume a culture that was beyond Israel's capacity even in the time of King Solomon. The account is vigorously given, in terms suggesting that it reproduces the Lord's instructions for creating the work, and its making is described stage by stage. Work which the Phoenicians, the most brilliant technicians of the Near East, had to be commissioned to carry out in the time of the Kings is here demanded of Israel itself: a people who did not even have settled homes, let alone workshops. It has long been assumed that this magnificent description is an idealization dating from the time of the prophets, imagining a central sanctuary for the past in the same way as Ezekiel's visionary temple imagined a sanctuary for the future. All the great concepts of the whole idea of God and the political unity of Israel in him are here related to the past. As a work of artistic imagination, the tabernacle is on a par with the real Temple of Jerusalem. It seems certain that it never really existed. Indeed, the tent of the tabernacle is not mentioned in any of the narratives in the books of Joshua, Samuel and Kings. The ark is always described as being carried on a litter, or on a cart: a small, portable shrine suitable for Israel's wandering in the desert. Religious feeling carries even greater weight if its inner profundities are focused upon something outwardly insignificant.

Nor could there have been any artistic foundations already present in the land Israel conquered. A considerable number of the most important pre-Israelite sites in Canaan have been more or less thoroughly excavated. Religious interests hoped to find evidence of Biblical truth buried in the ground. We have now come to know Taanach and Megiddo, Lachish and Gezer, Jericho, Beth-Shemesh and most recently Beth-Shean quite well. Nowhere, however, has a single work of architecture or pictorial art been found to compare with the Greek or Egyptian equivalents. In fact Canaan did not even have a style of its own. Its difficult position, situated as it was between Egypt and the great kingdoms of the Near East, made the long, narrow Canaanite territory more of a thoroughfare than a place where culture could develop. It had always been the subject of dispute or a battleground for its neighbours, never a breeding ground for culture. Politically speaking, it was a positive misfortune for Israel to have conquered the most explosive area in the Near East. Once there, Israel was never at peace, and foreign powers always had their eye on the country. Even Israel's settlement in Canaan and the founding of the state took place in the most difficult of circumstances and over an extremely long period. The people had invaded the territory with extraordinary energy, and now that we know something about the fortifications of Canaanite towns we can see why the conquest appeared miraculous, so that the land went in fear of Israel. However, no basis for the creation of art could be found in a land that had no national art of its own, but was only a conduit for currents flowing through it from all quarters of the compass.

The history of Canaan in the pre-Israelite period, i.e. in the second millennium BCE, was contingent upon its situation between two great powers, both of which coveted the territory: the Egyptians to the south and the Hittites to the north. The Hittite empire extended as far as the Lebanon: Kadesh on the Orontes was its southernmost fortress. Egypt, the land of culture *par excellence*, had always imported luxury goods from Syria, particularly cedar wood and cedar oil. Those links go back to the very beginnings of Egyptian history. With the founding of its new empire in the first third of the second millennium, Egypt began to expand beyond its borders and become a world power. Southern Palestine was its nearest and therefore its first target. Thutmes III passed through Canaan and conquered Syria in the course of fourteen campaigns, even taking its strong principal fortress of Megiddo on the road to Damascus where it reaches the plain of Jezreel, and capturing vast amounts of loot in the form of weapons and treasure in that city, which is described as 'worth more than the possession of a thousand other cities'. He catalogued his plunder in the list of his victories at Karnak, in the chief temple of his empire. He also overcame the Hittites, but they remained dangerous enemies and were never entirely vanquished. From then on Canaan was Egyptian territory until it was conquered by Israel.

However, it is typical of the international nature of the Egyptian empire that diplomatic correspondence was conducted in cuneiform script on clay tablets, in the Babylonian manner. The archives of Amenophis III and Amenophis IV found at El Amarna contain correspondence of this nature; the princes of Syria communicated with their Egyptian overlords in the same way, and so did the Hittite kings and the princes in Canaan when they wrote to each other, as we know from finds in Lachish and Taanach. These last letters already speak of great unrest in the land, feuding among the princes, rebellions, and possibly, even at this early date, of the Israelite invasion.

When Israel pressed forward it found a new enemy in the Philistines, its most dangerous opponents in the land. Their presence too was probably due to the Egyptians. The Philistines may well have been the dispersed remnants of the Sea Peoples of the Mediterranean who had ventured to attack Egypt, and after being repeatedly repulsed by the Ramessids

FIG. 6 The Canaanite cultic rock in the Omar Mosque, Jerusalem.

finally settled on the coast of Palestine. The prophet Amos still remembered that the Lord had brought them from Caphtor, which was probably Crete. They brought a new culture to Canaan, for they were an offshoot of the peoples who had created the brilliant pre-Greek culture of the Aegean Sea.

The art of Canaan faithfully reflects all these circumstances, graphically illustrating the cultural basis of historical events. The picture that emerges is one of a hotly disputed territory with an extremely primitive culture of its own, but remarkably rich in foreign imports. Indeed, the energy with which these foreign currents either deeply penetrated or simply flowed over the country is visible only in its acceptance or rejection of their structural ideas. That energy provides a fairly exact criterion by which to measure the force of historical events, how deep-reaching they were, and their cultural influence, and the finds made in excavations are very revealing for Palestine in particular.

First of all, Canaan must have been a noticeably religious place even before the Israelite conquest. Perhaps the most surprising fact revealed by the excavations was that the ancient inhabitants of Canaan, against whose idol-worship Israel was constantly being warned, actually worshipped idols less than did the Egyptians, Babylonians and Greeks. Seen from the inflexibly stern viewpoint of Old Testament religion, the cult practised in Canaan was certainly idolatry, but no Canaanite temple building and no cultic idols were found, only a vast quantity of amulets and tiny figures of later date, evidence of deep-rooted superstition in the minds of the people. The Canaanite cult itself obviously lacked images, contenting itself with sacrificial altars and the abstract symbols of large standing stones. Both were directly connected with nature and close to the earth. The surface of the rock itself was smoothed to make a sacrificial altar set apart from its surroundings and reached by hewn steps. Deep hollows were made to hold the sacrifices. Solid items such as meat and grain were burned in these hollows, and wine and oil were poured into the channels in the rock. Sacrificial altars of this kind have been found on many Canaanite sites, and one of them has retained its aura of sanctity for thousands of years: the Rock in Jerusalem over which the Muslims built the Omar Mosque, the holiest Islamic site in the Near East (fig. 6) .

The most interesting group of standing stones was in Gezer (fig. 7). Scholars sought with particular care for such monuments of Canaanite idolatry when they dug up Palestine, Bible in hand, much as Schliemann excavated Troy with Homer beside him, thus reading far more into their finds than the facts warranted. Every tall stone was regarded as a Canaanite cult object, but such stones often turned out later to be the foundations of oil presses, props for roofs or reinforcements for walls. In Gezer, however, they are certainly monuments, hewn standing stones rounded at the top. Eight of them stand upright above an ancient cave burial. Originally

FIG. 7 The row of standing stones in Gezer.

there were even more on this site: two stumps and an empty base show that three of the stelae were removed, and another, judging by the stone of which it was made, must have come from somewhere near Jerusalem, a point which again illustrates a historically familiar occurrence. It was very usual in antiquity for sacred objects and important monuments to be looted from enemy cities and displayed as a symbol of triumph in the conqueror's own capital. The most humiliating possible token of your enemy's defeat was to seize the symbols associated with the divinity he worshipped, thereby taking possession of the divinity itself and the protection it conferred. Odysseus, for instance, stole the Palladion, and some of the stelae of Assur are very like Canaanite standing stones. In the same way, the warriors of the tribe of Dan seized the images from the house of Micah, and the Philistines took the ark with the tables of the covenant. One cannot but notice how many Biblical customs coincide with those of Canaan. It was a pious custom from the time of the patriarchs onwards to erect memorial stones, and when Gideon sacrificed, laying the 'flesh and unleavened cakes' on a rock and pouring out the broth, he must have performed the rite on a sacrificial altar of the kind Israel found already present in Canaan. It was not easy for the invading nomadic people to oppose the culture of the earlier, sedentary culture of the land. The struggle for the victory of the clear-cut monotheism of Israel's ideology was a hard one and lasted a long time. We may take it for granted today, but it had difficulty in prevailing at a time when people formed their ideas from the evidence of their environment and were hardly capable of abstract thought, and among tribes who had existing, visible centres of worship all around on offer.

In line with the embattled conditions of Canaan, where cities had to be constantly on the watch and ever ready to fight, the fortified complexes of the time are remarkable, and indeed convey the strongest impression of all in the land. Urban layout was always ruled by considerations of security. All the cities were built on hills, and the natural slopes were made steeper with artificial fortifications which, despite the technical simplicity of the masons' techniques, were very well planned. Although these Canaanite cities were small, as one would expect in the cultural conditions of a time when agriculture and stock-breeding were the main means of livelihood – it has been estimated that around the middle of the second millennium the whole of Jericho was not much bigger than the single building of the Colosseum in Rome – the architectural achievement was none the less relatively great. Vast masses of rock and earth were shifted. Looking at these mighty fortresses, we can understand Israel's fear of these 'great, fortified' cities. In Megiddo, for instance, which Thutmes III managed to conquer but the tribe of Manasseh could not, the slope of the hill itself is made almost invulnerable by a terraced wall ten metres high. The lower part, itself further divided into three sections, was smoothed to make an impregnable glacis. No enemy could set foot on these clay fortifications, which were also extended by battlements to form strong defensive positions, and only above them does the real defensive wall rise, in two steep brick sections, the lower three metres and the upper rather over two metres high, with battlements some four metres wide. The whole complex is fitted with remarkable flexibility to the slope of the hill, making use of the hill itself as a defence.

FIG. 8 The Canaanite double wall, Jericho.

Jericho, the first city beyond the Jordan to be conquered by Israel, had fortifications of a different kind (fig. 8). They did not secure the slope of the hill but encircled the summit with two parallel walls. The outer wall was about one and a half metres wide, the main wall three and a half metres: the height in all must have been over five metres. There were towers at the corners, with wooden structures at the top to increase defensive power. It is interesting that these fortifications connect Jericho closely with Hittite culture. Although on a much smaller scale, they are laid out on the same system as the defensive wall of the Hittite capital of Boghazköy. Ideas of design reached Palestine from the Hittite kingdom, just as they arrived from Phoenicia later. In Shech sa'd, east of the Sea of Galilee, the area linked with the name of King Og of Bashan in the Bible, a stone lion still stands clearly visible in the cubic form of a block of stone, the remnant of a typical Hittite gateway of the end of the second millennium.

The houses of the Canaanite towns were purely utilitarian. Needs and

25

their fulfilment dominated this primitive culture so entirely that its dwelling houses say much less about it than its fortifications. Even buildings of some size, like the residences of the local kings of Taanach and Megiddo, are not remotely comparable with the palaces of the same period in Crete. The largest, in the capital city of Megiddo, was thirty-five metres long and thirty metres broad, and the individual rooms seldom measured more than four or five metres, so that they resembled rather modest living rooms of today. In general these rooms surrounded a large courtyard for utilitarian purposes, and indeed the rooms themselves were mainly utilitarian. The floors were made of compacted mud and the walls, built of brick on a foundation of rubble, were disproportionately thick in relation to the living area. Ceilings were flat roofs made of reeds and mud.

As for the houses of the ordinary people, they were modest to the point of poverty. It is true that the only details we have come from Jericho, since most archaeologists excavating in search of major items destroyed such houses without making so much as a ground plan first. These cities must have been unplanned collections of small houses, little more than huts, clinging together like cells in a honeycomb and intersected by small, crooked alleys. They crowded together within the city walls at the end of blind alleys. A single rectangular room generally seems to have been both living room and bedroom, with a small yard in front of it.

The Egyptian conquerors brought their own requirements and their own culture into this land, but one gets the clear impression that they regarded the place only as the object of power politics. They never really colonized it, or passed on to its people any of their own high intellectual and cultural standards. It is possible that they refrained from interfering with the country's internal structures out of clever foresight, to avoid having its inhabitants at their back as enemies. However that may be, the Egyptians merely passed through Canaan stationing garrisons there, and it never became a truly Egyptian country.

The latest excavations seem to identify Beth-Shean in the north of the Jordan plain as the most important Egyptian settlement in Canaan. Significant remains of a large Egyptian temple have been found there, as well as a fortress tower beautifully built of stone on a regular rectangular

FIGS 9 & 10 Small faience jars in the Egyptian style,
one in the shape of a lion, from Megiddo.

ground plan, with the local commander's house beside it. There was a huge granary in the courtyard of this house, probably to store provisions for the entire garrison. Lachish, the southern gateway to the country, also had an Egyptian temple of Hathor, and small Egyptian statuettes provide evidence of the worship of Egyptian divinities in Megiddo and Gezer. In a broader context, however, trade brought small works of Egyptian art into the country. Even small bronze statues have been found, and innumerable amulets, whose purpose may not have been understood at all by the Canaanites; it is possible that the women of Canaan simply wore them as jewellery, threaded on strings in rows. There were many images of Bes, the popular little half-animal dwarf god, the monkey god Thoth and the Eye of Horus. Delicate pendants were made from the meticulously shaped glossy blue faience of Egypt, and were of course immensely superior to any native handicrafts. Set beside the primitive Canaanite pots – coarse clay vessels with a naïve striped pattern – the imported Egyptian wares give the impression of being choice and undoubtedly expensive luxury goods. Canaan looked to Egypt as the Rococo art of all other European countries was later to look to Paris.

FIG. 11 Scarabs in a gold setting
from a tomb in Megiddo.

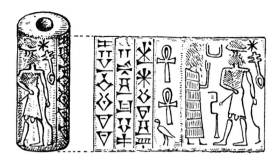

FIG. 12 Cylindrical seal from Taanach,
viewed sideways on, and as a panorama.

Megiddo has provided the richest finds, some of them very precious
pieces, yet they are only remnants of the quantities of plunder Thutmes
III seized there. They include little ointment jars shaped like animals,
three crouching lions, ducks, a monkey, a dove, and a very elegant green
pot with a brown pattern inside, all typical Egyptian ware (figs 9, 10).
The date when this trade was at its height can be precisely dated by the
enormous number of Egyptian scarabs found (fig. 11). These are small
seals in the shape of the sacred scarab beetle, mostly made of faience,
often bearing the name of a king on the underside. The series begins
with the twelfth dynasty, and the names most frequently found are those
of Thutmes, Amenophis III and Amenophis IV. This coincides exactly
with the time of the Egyptian campaigns, and thus of direct Egyptian
influence on Canaan. Such amulets were also imitated in Canaan itself, in
quantity and entirely without any understanding of their form or inscriptions. The influence of Babylonia, on the other hand, must have
been much less, for the only items found are two cylindrical seals, one in
Megiddo, one in its smaller sister city of Taanach (fig. 12). It is characteristic of Canaan's hybrid culture and the strength of Egyptian influence
that the second, the seal of one Atanahili son of Habsi, servant of Nergal,
which thus obviously belonged to a genuine Babylonian, bears some
misunderstood Egyptian hieroglyphs as well as cuneiform script and the
depiction of a god.

In the same way as monuments of Egyptian architecture in Palestine
occurred only sporadically and exerted no influence on the land itself,

FIG. 13 Canaanite pottery from Beth-Shemesh (Ain Shems).

Egyptian handicrafts were not influential either. Their designs left no deep impression on the country. The standard items found are ceramics of native Canaanite manufacture, naturally in considerable numbers, since large quantities of pottery were always needed and were buried in graves. Even in the third millennium BCE Canaan had some good pottery. Pots to contain liquids were rounded, as the hand originally shaped them, with a neck or handle added when necessary. The separate parts of the pots are not marked off from each other in any way, something that in itself would have amounted to artistic expression: the shape is the result of pure primitive feeling, not conscious decision. Brightly coloured decoration on the sides of the vessels was very popular. The finest painted vessels were found in Jerusalem itself, in the excavations of the mysterious site beside the Pool of Siloah. They are covered with a thin white layer to provide a uniform background for the painted decoration, and although that decoration consists only of quantities of parallel lines, the lines are so pleasingly distributed, with intersections and interruptions, that true works of art are created by these simple methods. Even at this point, technique and ornamentation were entirely different from the austerity of Egyptian art. Related ornamentation is found in the west, on the

Greek islands, and in Central Asia, but we do not know what links Palestine had with these lands in ancient times.

In the second millennium, the picture is entirely different. The vessels are now organically constructed and designed with an eye to the function of their various parts. They rise from a slender base, broaden into the main body of the vessel and become narrow at the neck, which now stands out prominently, as do curving handles which offer themselves to the grasp. The use of the potter's wheel can now be assumed, and with it the regularity of the curve of a clay pot and the uniform thickness of its sides. This was the period at which Canaan became aware of culture and extended its requirements and its trade network. Egyptian imports have already been discussed, but they remained foreign goods. The ceramics of Canaan were closer to the pottery of Cyprus than any other known ceramics, but we do not know whether that island was the source of its own very diverse shapes and styles or whether it was merely an outpost of Phoenicia. It was probably part of an artistic area extending over much of the Near East, displaying a unity of style that reached the artistic province of Canaan, very likely by the same routes as those that took Phoenician artists to the court of King Solomon. Plenty of good pottery of all Phoenician styles came to Canaan and was imitated there. A cave burial in Ain Shems, containing the dead man's entire and lavish household equipment, shows how diverse the style could be, with a special shape of vessel for every purpose, none of them merely commonplace in design (fig. 13). Potters with the gift of good taste found new ideas for every purpose. Typical items include small, squat pots and pointed pitchers with high shoulders and a crooked neck; crude imitations of these Phoenician ceramics are the most frequently found products of Canaan's own potters' kilns.

Yet the trade of Canaan in the second millennium must have reached further afield, connecting the land with all cultures of the eastern Mediterranean. The most creative of all these was the culture of Crete, and its brilliance was reflected even in the Homeric hymns and the Greek myths of King Minos. Its palaces were buildings of great magnificence, their walls adorned with impressionistic frescos depicting subjects from real

FIGS 14 & 15 Philistine pottery from Beth-Shemesh (Ain Shems).

life with great vigour. Their goldsmiths made vessels showing scenes in realistic relief on their sides, and there were ceramics of the greatest elegance, with images of marine animal life depicted in shining dark glaze. So far as we know none of these items found their way to Canaan except for the ceramics. Many Canaanite graves contained slender vases rising in a graceful curve from a pointed foot, and round stirrup jars with handles elegantly designed for the grip of the human hand.

This style had a cruder offshoot in Palestine itself. It mainly takes the shape of the big-bellied pitcher, typically ornamented with friezes surrounding the shoulders of the vessel like architectonic borders (figs 14, 15). These friezes have sections of plain lines alternating with sections depicting animals, mostly birds, in rhythmic succession, and resembling the triglyph and metope friezes of Greek temples. The pictures are not as lively as the Cretan depictions of animals, and instead are so stylized that they seem to have become mere ornamentation of the vessel, whose shape takes precedence over any kind of free creativity. Although these ceramics descend from Aegean forms they cannot be classed with either Aegean or Cypriot pottery. This is a more recent, independent style.

There is in fact one Palestinian people who could have made these ceramics, the people who gave their name to 'Palestine', the Philistines.

The Bible knew that they came from Crete. Moreover, most ceramics of this kind are found in the old Philistine cities: Tell es Safi, which may have been ancient Gad, Gezer and more particularly Ain Shems, probably Beth-Shemesh on the borders of Philistine country and the first place to which the ark of the covenant came on its return to Israelite territory. On the other hand, there is no pottery like this in northern Palestine, Taanach and Megiddo. Again, Philistine culture used Egyptian models for its more valuable utensils, and in fact the Philistines must have been very rich. Their sacrificial offerings of gold to the ark sound like a genuine tradition. The only places where precious metals have been found are Philistine graves. The tombs of Gezer, where the dead had silver plaques bound over their mouths in a manner reminiscent of customs on the Greek seaboard, contained a wealth of material: jewellery, a mirror still in its case, a silver jug, dish and spoon, all in slender designs derived from the flower shapes of Egyptian art. A second treasure of the same kind, a flower-shaped drinking vessel and a ladle with a handle modelled on the swimming woman of Egyptian ointment pots, has recently been found in Beth-Paleth, the home of the Philistines and of King David's bodyguard.

At this point the contrast between Israel and the culture of the land it conquered becomes evident. It was as clear-cut a contrast as can be imagined. Artistically, Canaan was very passive, subject to foreign incursions and foreign influences. However, the way such influences infiltrated the country, each of them controlling certain distinct cultural and territorial areas, was not just chance or coincidence. The basis of life and art alike was Asian, and probably closely related to Hittite culture. Phoenician culture was heir to the Hittites, in art and in its power over Palestine. This fact in itself was an obstacle to Babylonian influence, for the Hittites, who were more powerful at the time, barred the way to Babylon. Great quantities of Egyptian goods came into the country, however, and they must have been widely coveted. This contrast between north and south coincides with another, between east and west. The Philistines had come to the coastal areas from the west, foreign in their arms and armour (Goliath's armour is very precisely described), foreign in their burial customs and European art forms. Shortly after the arrival of the Philistines – probably around 1250 – the Israelites invaded the country. And in Jericho, the first city they conquered in Canaan and always one of the most orthodox, not an amulet nor a single idol of bronze or clay has been found. Not a scarab, not a cylindrical seal has surfaced from Canaanite houses or the thin Israelite cultural stratum over them. The finds from excavations illustrate the Biblical account very graphically.

CHAPTER TWO

The Time of the Kings

THE GLORY of all Jewish history is the period of the first three
kings, at the turn of the second to the first millennium BCE. It
made the nomadic people of the children of Israel a political
power to be reckoned with in the Middle East. Historically, the Biblical
account is extremely interesting. Nowhere else can we follow so clearly
the stages of development from a merely tribal community, its individual
members living side by side and only occasionally assembling in a body,
to a state with a uniform administrative system. Nowhere else do we
acquire such clear insights into the people who contributed to this process,
their motives, their conscious will and their unconscious drives.

The rise took place in three stages under three leaders. The first two of
them, Saul and David, were genuine kings from the people, chosen by
Samuel, the spiritual leader of the nation. The last, Solomon, was David's
son who succeeded by inheritance, and it is with him that political decline
in fact set in.

Saul (c.1030–1010) was the first to unite the inner strength of the nation.
The idea of a unified state grew and flourished under his leadership.
However, there was still no established organization, and he did not
succeed in securing the border defences. Basically, conditions were still
what they had been in the time of the Judges, and the people were still
too rustic to feel any artistic needs.

David (c.1010–970), undoubtedly the cleverest leader in ancient Israelite
history, was the real architect of the state, and at the same time he took
the first step towards Israel's artistic achievements. Having grown up during
the struggles against the Philistines, he was the first to see that his people

lacked not strength but unity, and unity was what he gave them. He made his city of Jerusalem a national centre. His decision to build a palace there, and even more his second decision to bring the ark to Jerusalem, were crucial to the whole history of Israel. It now had a political centre which was identical with its religious centre. The Biblical account makes it clear that the king did not take his decision easily. It went against all popular customs and meant a final break with the sacrosanct traditions of the nomadic period. However, David ventured to take it, thereby making Israel, its religion, and the kingdom a community with roots in one place, Jerusalem. His appointment of a bodyguard that would be unconditionally at his command, in addition to the levy of the tribes, was an equally bold and necessary decision for the leader of a young state that must be constantly wary. It is significant, however, that he did not yet venture to build the temple, merely preparing a tent for the ark of the covenant. The reason lay in religious scruples: what is sacred must not be modernized, is immutable, a law unto itself. As for David's house, it cannot have been a very artistic structure. The Bible merely says that the Phoenician Hiram King of Tyre (Zor) built it for him, mentioning only 'carpenters and masons', and describing it very briefly by comparison with the long accounts of Solomon's buildings. As the Bible is a very reliable source, it may be assumed that the remarkable point about the house was that it was built at all, and Israel in fact had no craftsmen capable of doing the work. One can see why King Hiram of Tyre was ready to accommodate King David, who was a dangerous neighbour; he had extended his power to Damascus and was lord of Edom, Moab and Amman. At this time Israel was the most powerful nation between Egypt and Mesopotamia.

Solomon (c.970–930), the heir to David's kingdom, built a genuinely royal culture on these firm foundations. This was the first time an Israelite leader had had the security and leisure to turn his mind to works of art. Solomon's whole personality, which is sharply delineated in the Bible, tended towards intellectual activity. He was king rather than warrior, since he no longer had to make conquests, only to secure conquests already made. David's son, who grew up in the royal palace, was spared his father's own difficult youth. He was brought up not to war but to pleasure, and must have been the first genuinely cultured man among his people: all the accounts of his wisdom, poetic skill and architectural achievements lead one to that conclusion.

Yet his was the most difficult task in the whole history of the founding of the nation. As soon as Israel ceased to be a landless nomadic tribe, without economic needs or any claim to culture, it necessarily had to define both its political and its intellectual positions in relation to surrounding peoples. The Israelites were now living on a busy highway, trade and transport were factors to be reckoned with, foreign ideas came in across the borders, and while this was an inevitable development it was also dangerous, both inside and outside the country. Outside, Israel's possession of the land caused hostility; its great neighbours looked covetously at Palestine now that it was Israelite, just as they had when it was Canaanite. Inside, traditionalists regarded this new flowering of culture as backsliding and decadence, with some reason, for the austere formal repertory of ancient Israel and indeed of the Canaanite farmers could not meet modern demands for luxury and art. Solomon therefore turned to Phoenicia, and the art he created was essentially non-national and irreligious, for the designs and ornamentation of his buildings were all foreign and were basically derived from foreign religious feeling. Although Solomon did not adopt that religious feeling for cultic purposes, there was a great temptation to see the higher culture he strove for as existing in foreign religion as well. Solomon was known to be prone to such ideas. Finally, the balance sheet in material terms was unsatisfactory too: Solomon was so deeply in debt to the king of Tyre that he had to cede considerable amounts of territory to placate him.

In terms of art history, Solomon's royal buildings brought Israel into the stylistic area of the Near East. They were the first great architectural work of Israel. His temple and his palace, important in both their design and their decoration, were the nation's greatest cultural expression, and they remained so for a long period.

They must have made an extraordinary impression on the people who saw the nation's inner significance set before their eyes for the first time.

The buildings would have appeared miraculous to them, and amazement echoes through all the accounts, in line with the prominence given to their precise description in the first book of Kings and the books of Chronicles. It is by far the best architectural description from early antiquity to have been preserved – the period was just at the turn from the second to the first millennium – and of great importance in the history of art.

Yet it is extremely difficult to form any real idea of what the buildings looked like. The text employs many technical terms current at the time, but entirely mysterious to us, and even where the meaning is not in doubt the actual appearance of the buildings is imprecise. The descriptions of the pillars Jachin and Boaz, the decoration of the walls in the temple, and the ten stands of brass seem perfectly clear but are not really clear at all, since we do not know just what structures are indicated by the many words expended on them, and even some obviously very close analogies among Phoenician finds do not permit identification. Consequently, piety and scholarship have made repeated attempts to reconstruct the temple and the palace, down to their smallest utensils, and no one reconstruction has resembled any of the others. Even the best account of a chronicler describing buildings that stood before his very eyes is not exact enough to convey more than a vague idea to a reader who has nothing but the text. Every period has unconsciously regarded the Bible in terms of its own ideas, translating its descriptions into the taste and formal structures of its time. Textual problems have often been ascribed to the long series of copyists at work between the original text and its present, Masoretic form, and the result has been emendations and conjecture. It is a fact that the texts of these accounts is not uniformly reliable. There are many repetitions and obscurities. However, they are sufficient for us to form a general idea of the buildings, and even draw some conclusions about their style.

The temple Solomon spent seven years building was a long rectangle (fig. 16); the Bible gives its measurements as sixty cubits long and twenty cubits broad (a cubit being about half a metre). It rose towards the back, from the entrance to the inner sanctuary. The walls were made of hewn stone. Inside, the hard stone surfaces were hidden by a lining of wooden

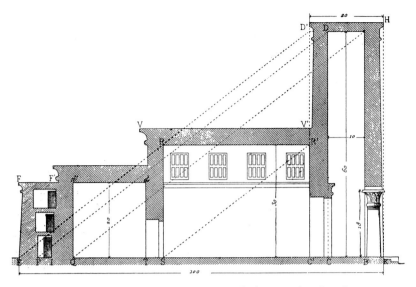

Fig. 16 Attempt at a reconstruction of the temple of Solomon, by M. de Vogüé, lengthwise section. (Uncertain in many details.)

panelling covered with gold, and there was a frieze of cherubim, palms and flowers in relief. The temple had three main areas. The porch was only ten cubits long, and was thus quite broad. (If it had really been of the enormous height given in Chronicles, it would have looked like one of the vast pylons of ancient Egypt.) Next came the *hekal*, the cult area, which was forty cubits long, and the holy of holies, the *debir*, twenty cubits long, broad and high, where the ark of the covenant stood beneath the gilded wooden statues of two cherubim. Wooden doors, also covered with gold, separated the *hekal* and *debir*. Around the temple – whether outside it or inside we are not told, but obviously outside – ran a series of subsidiary wooden rooms three storeys high, the lowest being five cubits broad, the middle storey six cubits and the third storey seven cubits; the effect may have been of a projecting corbel of the kind often found in wooden architectural structures, particularly in Oriental galleries.

The entrance was flanked by two monumental bronze pillars. They were cast by Huram-abi the Phoenician, and the idea behind them is undoubtedly Phoenician too. They cannot have held up the entrance; they were not structural parts of the building but symbols, illustrating

Fig, 17 Clay model of a Phoenician temple
from Dali on Cyprus.

religious ideas with which Israel was unacquainted, so that the Israelites took the pillars to be a natural part of a temple. A clay model of a temple from Cyprus illustrates the same feature, pillars flanking an entrance (fig. 17); as usual in small works, it shows the type rather than any individuality, but it helps us to understand the Biblical description. The capitals are lily-shaped, with a long boss (the Biblical 'knop') erect in the centre. The Biblical description of the pillars mentions both these features, without saying anything about their more intricate ornamentation.

This type of temple was still found in Syria in Hellenistic times, and is not Israelite. It is the same design described by Lucian as that of the temple of the Syrian goddess in Bambyke, including the two monumental pillars, which he calls phalli, identifying them as sexual symbols. We know nothing about the origin of the design. It has been claimed that it was quite an advanced ground plan, a Hittite long rectangle with a broad *hekal*, in line with the change from a Babylonian to an Assyrian type of temple. The Assyrian ground plan does correspond closely to the plan of Solomon's temple, and it is quite possible that the form reached Assyria on the same western Asiatic currents as those that also brought Phoenician bronze shields, ivory work and Near Eastern ornamentation.

The royal palace was a more complicated piece of architecture, thirteen years in the building, almost twice as long as it took to build the temple. It must have been a very extensive complex of more or less self-contained separate buildings, some of them at least arranged around a courtyard which was probably also the courtyard of the temple, as in Assyria. There were at least four buildings: the poetically named 'house of the forest of Lebanon', the throne room, the king's dwelling house and the house of his chief wife, Pharaoh's daughter. The description in Kings I is merely an enumeration, and does not tell us exactly what lay or did not lie under a particular roof. It certainly does not allow us to draw up a ground plan. An attempt has recently been made to suggest that all of the king's palace was accommodated in two storeys of a single building, a hypothesis which contradicts not only the text but all the customs of ancient Oriental architecture, not to speak of the cramped discomfort of such a building. Such spatial concentration was scarcely possible even in a Baroque palace.

Only one part of the building is described in detail, the house of the forest of Lebanon, and this interesting and historically important account leaves us only able to guess at those conclusions we cannot draw because the description of the complex as a whole is so vague.

If we keep to the text at this point, leaving aside conjectures or 'emendations', a clear picture emerges. The building was a wooden pillared hall a hundred cubits long, fifty cubits broad and thirty cubits high, i.e. as tall as the temple and considerably broader. It must have been open to the elements: the text mentions no walls, and had they existed it would surely have mentioned them here, as with the temple. Reconstructions from the information provided are very arbitrary (fig. 18). The pillars (their number is not given) stood in four rows, forming three naves. The upper storey corresponded to this substructure and contained three rows of chambers, fifteen to each row and leading into each other, door opposite door, the carpentry of the door and window frames consisting of squared posts. The description is so important because in the course of nature all ancient wooden buildings have been lost, either destroyed by fire or simply rotting away, and this is the earliest account of a type of architecture that suddenly emerges in the east five hundred years later, but which certainly had a long previous history. The house of the forest of Lebanon is built

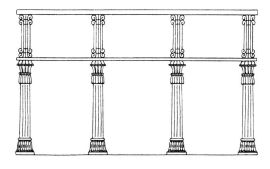

FIG. 18 The house of the forest of Lebanon.
The author's attempt at a reconstruction: cross-section and ground plan.
The pillars are designed on the Persian model (not confirmed).

to the same architectural concept as the so-called *apadana*, the halls of
the Persian palaces in Susa and Persepolis. Sarre, their historian, assumes
that the stone pillars had developed from a wooden form, and the square
ground plan was preceded by a rectangular one, exactly like the plan of
Solomon's house of the forest of Lebanon. It must have been extremely
close to the original type, even in the details, for it cannot be coincidence
that the Persian pillars also bore a superstructure of squared posts which
look as if they were intended to bear an upper storey. It is also interesting, if not surprising in the post-Persian period, that the word *apadana*

41

itself appears in the text of Ecclesiasticus, as a loan-word for 'hall'.

The Biblical account, very exact at this point too, gives precise details of the different shares of Israelites and Phoenicians in the building work. Naturally enough it says nothing about the similarity of the layout to other Oriental works of architecture; as in the description of the buildings of any religion, it regards the special cultic characteristics of the temple as the important point, not its resemblance to any other buildings. In fact the Phoenicians' share in the building was not so very great. Only the timbers were erected on the spot by Hiram's Phoenician workmen, while the Israelites whom Solomon had levied to do forced labour worked in the stone quarries and transported the materials overland. The masonry and carpentry of the buildings also seem to have been the work of Israelite craftsmen. However, it is particularly interesting that they had obviously mastered the most striking of the ornamental techniques involved, covering the walls and the statues of the cherubim in the holy of holies with gold.

Two passages describe this technique precisely; the items represented were carved from wood and then covered with a thin layer of gold leaf, which could be moulded precisely to the wooden carving. This technique of embossed ornamentation was still current in the Middle Ages, and in antiquity it was employed throughout the area of Phoenician artistic influence.

Providing the utensils for the temple, work for a skilled craftsman, was a different matter. Where there was no underlying wooden shape to have metal applied to its surfaces, items had to be cast, an art beyond the Israelites. The Bible emphasizes that the cast metal work was done by one Hiram or Huram-abi of Tyre, who must have been a free craftsman, for his work is mentioned separately from that of the forced labourers, and is allotted high praise. He worked at a place on the Jordan plain which had suitable sand; its location is given precisely. The only way to make free-standing works of art was by this technique of casting, smelting and founding, which required great skill and experience, and centuries of the practice of the craft were a pre-requisite. The only metalwork of which Israel was capable was working with cold sheet metal.

FIG. 19 Mobile bronze stand from Larnaka, Cyprus.
Berlin, the Museum.

For everything in the temple, Solomon used the most precious material that was suitable, so these different techniques were necessary. Bronze, i.e. copper alloy, was used, as it was throughout this cultural area at the time, and so was gold: bronze for monumental items and the minor utensils for divine service, gold for utensils immediately serving the divinity.

FIG. 20 Stylized tree between cherubim (detail from FIG. 19).

Consequently the altar, the table for the showbread, the sacrificial implements and the ten candlesticks with their accessories were made of gold. Solomon's temple did not have a branched candelabrum. Indeed, seven as a symbolic number is not found at this early Israelite period; sets of items come in tens and twelves. It is interesting that the Biblical account mentions no ornamentation at all on the most precious of all the implements used in the holiest acts of devotion, whereas it positively luxuriates in description of the decoration elsewhere. Obviously these implements really were plain in design, and even at Solomon's court craftsmen fought shy of adorning them with any image or figure.

The two huge architectonic pillars Jachin and Boaz and the 'molten sea' (a large laver or basin) five cubits high and standing on twelve oxen were made of bronze. It is expressly stated that the oxen were looking outward, three to each point of the compass. Unlike the gilded cherubim of the temple, they must therefore have been free-standing statues. The ten mobile bronze stands for the basins were more in the nature of utensils.

FIG. 21 Phoenician decorative bronze shield, found in the palace of Nimrod in
Assyria. The representations of oxen probably resemble the oxen
carrying the 'molten sea' on the temple of Solomon.

And while we can form only a vague idea of the appearance of the oxen
supporting the molten sea, stands from Cyprus extremely like the strikingly
detailed Biblical description have been found; the finest, from Larnaka, is
in the Antiquarium in Berlin (fig. 19). It is a kind of rectangular table on
tall legs with wheels, making it mobile. It has a circular ring on top
where the basin, now lost, once stood. Spirals are a recurrent motif. Two
sphinxes with a tree trunk shaped like a pillar between them stand face to
face on each of the sides (fig. 20). The whole stand gives us a good idea
of the Phoenician and thus of the Solomonic style. It is much decorated
and not particularly tectonic: the legs are thin and stick-like, the struts
more like linked tendrils than functional bearers, the borders are shaped
like twisted cords or spirals, the frame of the stand full of decorative
figures. Everything about it is thin, delicate, filigree-like. The ornamental

45

work is very stylized. The question now is, did what the Bible describes as cherubim and palm trees actually look like the figures on the sides of the Larnaka stand? The idea that by cherubim the Bible meant angels, winged messengers of God, is a late, even a Christian assumption. We can gather nothing about their appearance from the Bible except that they were probably figures of demonic appearance. We must see them as something similar to the lions and oxen mentioned by the Bible in the same passage, and take a rather closer look at the entire artistic world of the time.

The fact that Solomon turned to Tyre for his artistic commissions rather than Egypt, to whose ruler he was related by marriage, was not merely the policy of a good neighbour, but shows that Israel had entered the ranks of the great cultural peoples of the eastern basin of the Mediterranean. Not only were the products of Phoenician craftsmanship those he could most easily acquire, they were the best and indeed the only international wares of their time. Homer speaks of them with the same enthusiasm as the Bible does. Phoenician dishes and shields such as those with which Solomon furnished the house of the forest of Lebanon were found all over the ancient world (fig. 21). Their area of distribution extended from Assyria and Armenia in the east to Greece, Etruria and Gaul. Many of those found have Phoenician names scratched on them, perhaps as a trade mark, and one of them, in the holiest place in Greece, Olympia, even bears an Aramaic inscription. Mobile stands for basins came into this category of export goods. Furniture such as Solomon's throne with its ivory carvings of fabulous beasts was made by Phoenicians for the palaces of Assyrian kings.

Phoenicia devised an international and very adaptable style for such goods, combining all the stylistic forms of the east, and marketable in any country. It was a style that became magnificently imaginative just because it had no inhibitions about adopting and merging ideas. Stylized cattle, lions, griffins and sphinxes occupy the same frieze. In mythological friezes, ancient Hittite fabulous animals, Egyptian kings and gods mingle with Assyrian demons. The female divinities, presumably figures of Astarte, are derived from the related Egyptian goddess Hathor, shown with two

FIG. 22 (*left*) Mould to make images of Astarte, from Megiddo.
FIG. 23 (*right*) Impression of seal from Megiddo, white limestone.

long plant stems growing into her hands from the pillars decorated with lilies, lotus and papyrus among which she stands. The king of Egypt, wearing an Assyrian robe, can be seen fighting a winged griffin. Friezes of a narrative nature combine Assyrian sieges of cities with the idyllic agricultural scenes of Egyptian tombs.

The descriptions in the first book of Kings are not the only evidence we have that this style reached Palestine: excavations have confirmed the fact. Little figures of Astarte have been found in large numbers. She appears once in Gezer, probably still in Canaanite times, clad in full Egyptian regalia with horns, feathers and the uraeus headdress. A clay mould found in Megiddo, which incidentally proves that such figurines were locally manufactured, made it possible to produce shapes of her in the form of a naked idol, with the typical locks of Hathor and long-stemmed lotus flowers in her hands (fig. 22). This stereotype is repeated over and over again, degenerating to a point where it is scarcely recognizable. Another type shows the same naked goddess with great emphasis on sensuality, her hands grasping her breasts. The uninterrupted flow of Phoenician influence into Canaan can be traced through these finds, from the time when Phoenician art was still adopting almost purely Egyptian forms for its divinities, up to the emergence of an misunderstood and degenerate hybrid type. The oldest images of Astarte still belong to the Canaanite period before Israel came into the land, while the later examples must belong to the time of the Kings, a period for which the cult of the goddess is attested (and much deplored). No images of male deities such as Baal have been found; however, there are frequent figures of oxen, as there are throughout the area of Phoenician artistic influence, and as they appear associated with Solomon's molten sea. Palestine also knew the fabulous animal hybrids of Phoenician art. A particularly fine piece of work has been found in Megiddo: an oval seal of white limestone carved with a precision of design and a well-balanced division of the surface which shows great skill in intaglio work (fig. 23). Two griffins, winged lions with the heads of birds, stand symmetrically in the centre, one on each side of a mythological tree originally connected with a Hittite royal hieroglyph. The small semi-circular areas above and below provide a lively accompaniment to this statuary motif, their curves skilfully filled by animals in conflict, an ancient Oriental theme known in both Egypt and Mesopotamia. In the lower area of the seal, a lion has leaped on the back of an ibex which is defending itself with its horns – an idea originating in ancient stellar myths but shown here in a very realistic manner, and similarly the small hare fleeing from a vulture in the upper area becomes something almost like an animal fable.

This imaginative Phoenician world, a great melting-pot of eastern concepts, had an immense effect on Israel, as it did on all the young nations of the time as they sought formal expression for their undeveloped ideas of their gods. Etruscan graves are full of images of Phoenician origin. The Greeks constructed their first pictorial representations of divinities on Phoenician foundations. The vase paintings of the Greek Corinthian style, adopted by the earliest Athenian vase painters, and much of the ornamentation of the most ancient architectural monuments of Greece, are simply translations of Phoenician pictorial ideas. Sirens and sphinxes, chimaeras and griffins are Greek names for various species of fantastic Phoenician hybrids, and some of these are actually Semitic loan-words not originally native to the Greek language. The Greek stem *gryph*, which in western European languages has become English 'griffin' and 'gryphon', French *griffon*, German *Greif*, etc., is undoubtedly identical with the *k'rub* of the Bible, incorrectly transliterated today as 'cherub'. It is among such fantastic animals, whose demonic significance echoes on as late as the prophets, that we must seek the models for the figures Solomon brought to Israel. It is no coincidence that the stand from Larnaka shows them in the same place as did Solomon's mobile stands. His artists were acquainted with this pictorial way of thinking, but to Israel it must have seemed like wild imagination, and its full symbolic significance cannot have been understood, although it served to adorn temples and implements in situations where the Phoenicians were accustomed to it. It is interesting to note that the Bible draws no distinctions at all between the various species of animal demons, and speaks of cherubim (probably comprising all the creatures called in Greece by such names as griffin and sphinx, chimaera and siren) in the same breath as it speaks of lions and oxen. Like the two pillars in front of the temple, they were accepted ornamental themes in this artistic context. That very fact makes it difficult, among the large number of Phoenician motifs, to identify those mentioned in the Bible as 'wreaths of chain work', 'lily work', 'gourds', 'pomegranates', and other more or less distinct subjects. It is certain that they were all stylized and had been reduced from natural to architectural forms, and the palm trees too would have resembled the stylized tree between the Larnaka cherubim. Although relatively few separate decorative motifs are mentioned, there must have been a rich diversity of forms.

Conflict centring on this world of imagery continued through the centuries of the time of the Kings. Basically, it had nothing to do with art history but was social, inherent in the contrast between the people, themselves very poor, and the demands of their rulers, although those demands were unavoidable because they served politics in the longer term. The outward splendour was much less important than its inner significance. It is interesting that the kingdom split after Solomon's death not because of any religious dispute but through reluctance to provide the *corvée* of forced labour which Rehoboam in his own turn demanded. It has always been difficult to accustom a nomadic tribe to state organization: it has to give up much of its freedom and autonomy, but only thus can a collection of individuals become a nation and a state.

Even the time of the Judges was a period in Israel when everyone went his own way. Israel was not used to taking orders, being heavily taxed, or recruited for forced labour. Solomon had to demand all these things if he was to ensure Israel's existence as a state, and if that state was to have prosperity and culture, but the people grudged his demands and rebelled against his son.

At first the division into two kingdoms, the northern kingdom of Israel with its centres in Samaria and Bethel and the southern kingdom of Judah with its centre in Jerusalem, meant a decline in the popular power David and Solomon had amassed. Naturally the kings of the new kingdoms tried to secure themselves within their boundaries. Rehoboam put much energy into extending the cities of his southern kingdom, particularly Lachish, its southernmost fortress. It may also have been Rehoboam who built the remarkable rectangular halls on stone pillars in Lachish and the old fortifications that have been excavated in Tell Sandahanneh, the old city of Mareshah; there is evidence that he built in both places. However, he was not strong enough to repel the invasion of the Egyptian king Shishak, who reached Jerusalem and robbed Solomon's temple of its golden utensils and shields, which Rehoboam replaced by bronze ones. Cities of the northern kingdom appear on the list of Shishak's victories in Karnak as well. When the kingdom divided, it had destroyed its own power to defend itself.

However, the extent of the damage was not immediately apparent. The glory of Israel by no means died with Solomon, and the northern kingdom in particular flourished at the beginning of the ninth century. The Omrid dynasty (mentioned in Assyrian inscriptions, and the first to win respect abroad) sought to ensure its domination very much in the spirit of Solomon. Omri himself made Samaria the new centre of his kingdom, and his warrior son Ahab, who restored diplomatic connections abroad by his marriage to a Phoenician princess and his toleration of foreign culture, was probably responsible for more architecture than anyone else in the northern kingdom. Remains of his buildings of hewn stone have been found in Samaria above what is left of Omri's foundation, although we cannot be sure whether they are remains of the citadel or

FIG. 24 Part of Hiel's wall, Jericho.

of the temple of Baal. In Ahab's reign, Jericho was rebuilt by Hiel of Bethel. This rebuilding was a huge work, constructed above the ruined city, almost a rebuilding of the hill itself. The books of Kings speak of it almost with awe: 'He [Hiel] laid the foundation thereof in Abiram his firstborn, and set up the gates thereof in his youngest son Segub, according to the word of the Lord, which he spake by Joshua the son of Nun.'

Despite Joshua's curse on anyone who rebuilt Jericho, the place was too important and its situation on the Jordan too dominant, providing access as it did to the mountainous country of Palestine, to be allowed to lie in ruins for ever. On the other hand, the task was extraordinarily difficult, for the ruins of the old city still rose above the rubble left after its destruction, and in places remnants of the city wall rose to a height of seven metres.

Hiel set energetically about his task. He made what amounted to a new site on which to build his city, apparently razing and levelling the entire old town to provide new, flat ground upon which to build. This made the new Jericho even more dominant. Retaining walls went down the slope, securing the artificial hillside (fig. 24); steps, a considerable number of which have been excavated, now led downhill from the plateau on which the city stood to the new wall. Steps of this kind occurred in Hittite architecture, and while they may have served to transport building materials to the site they also had a defensive purpose. Getting up and down the hill quickly and at many points was important, for the new defensive wall no longer secured just the plateau but the whole slope. Fitting closely to the line of the hillside, it surrounded it with a regularity which makes the Canaanite wall look crude and clumsy. This superior skill is also evident in the structure itself. A layer of clay concrete, a very strong load-bearing material, supports a stone wall which not only slopes but traces a rounded course in a regular, extensive curve which makes it almost impossible to climb. It is up to five and a half metres high, built in two sections and in the Cyclopean style of ancient masonry, using massive blocks with smaller stones fitted between them to create a firm mass. The defensive wall proper stood on this substructure. It was made of mud bricks, was two metres broad, and today it is still up to 2.40 metres tall, but it must have been considerably higher when first built. A functional structure thus became an architectural work of monumental power. The builders understood that structural unity would serve the purpose better than building what was merely necessary, and the wall's superiority to its Canaanite predecessor shows how greatly architectural style had developed.

The same Cyclopean masonry was employed in a large building in Jericho near the well. It may have been Hiel's own house. The remains preserved and now excavated show that it was a building consisting of two disproportionately narrow rooms (10.50 metres long and 3.70 metres wide) lying one behind the other, with two more behind them covering the same area in all. The ground plan is therefore a broad one, in line with Hittite architecture. Even in Canaanite times, Jericho was notable for its tendency towards the Hittite style, as opposed to western Palestine, and the same stylistic feeling is perceptible in what has been excavated of

FIG. 25 Ruins of Jewish houses, Jericho.

the private houses of the city at the time of the Kings (fig. 25). Built soon after the construction of Hiel's unified design, sometimes even built above his steps, these houses too are set behind rectangular courtyards with their broader sides facing forward and they are far larger and more impressive than the former huddle of houses behind the Canaanite city wall. So far, however, nothing like the fine dressed stone buildings of the royal cities has been found in Jericho.

This may not be just chance. It could be symptomatic of a stylistic development such as we must certainly assume took place throughout the long period of the Kings, although no actual evidence has yet been found. The nation served its technical apprenticeship on Solomon's great buildings, and this base of knowledge was broadened under his successors. As usual in economic history, the growth of trade in Israel led to the rise of a property-owning, luxury-loving merchant class. It developed the architecture that provided its houses, and created a market for works of

FIG. 26 Corner of a building from the time of the Kings in Jericho.

craftsmanship. At the same time, however, social differences became more marked, and dangers unknown in the old peasant society of Israel emerged. When the prophets made themselves spokesmen for the oppressed they felt it their religious duty, regarding themselves as the upholders of the nation's true tradition, a situation not without its historical parallels. 'Forasmuch therefore,' says Amos, 'as your treading is upon the poor, and ye take from him burdens of wheat: ye have built houses of hewn stone, but ye shall not dwell in them; ye have planted pleasant vineyards, but ye shall not drink wine of them,' and he goes on to speak of beds of ivory, feasting and music. The courts of his time, of Jeroboam II in Israel, whose summer and winter palaces are described, and of Uzziah in Judah, were the places where this luxury was indulged in.

At this time the northern kingdom extended to Damascus and Hamat, the frontiers of Assyria, and there was peace between it and the southern kingdom, which was also at the height of its power.

Part of a palace of superb dressed stone has been excavated in Megiddo (fig. 26). It must surely once have been an architectural masterpiece, and

Fig. 27 Capital from Megiddo, of the time of the Kings.

as a ruin it is still impressive. Judging by the finds, it must have been one of Jeroboam II's residences. Attempts have been made to ascribe the building to Solomon, but he maintained only a steward in Megiddo.

A tower-like three-roomed building, of architectural precision hitherto quite unknown in Canaan, stood on top of the hill. It had a great courtyard no less than sixty metres long and surrounded by very solid dressed stone walls. Unlike the roughly shaped substructures built of piled, crudely dressed small stones in the western citadel of Taanach, the palace in Megiddo was genuine, structurally expressive architecture. The ground plan is completely rectangular, and the very well hewn limestone blocks are precisely adjusted. The method seems to have been to erect tall cornerstones, laying stones between them in both directions – runners and binders – and fixing them with mortar. Unlike the remains in Taanach these were walls in themselves, not intended to carry a superstructure, and bore only a low course of bricks on top. The rooms were about three metres high with wooden ceilings, like Solomon's buildings in Jerusalem, and the floor was paved with clay tiles. A taste for luxury had developed: people were no longer content to walk on uneven trodden mud floors. The appointments of the building were probably very elegant. It is as good as certain that an Egyptian-style cavetto with a cornice was part of it, along with a finely worked capital that has been found (fig. 27) and the remains of the uprights and beams of a hall – and we may

FIG. 28 (*left*) Seal of Shema ebed Jeroboam, from Megiddo.
FIG. 29 (*right*) Impression of the seal of Asaph, from Megiddo.

remember that a distinction was drawn between the king's winter and summer palaces. Such designs might be expected in Palestine, and the Egyptian style of the beams even suggests Mesopotamian forms, not just Phoenician design of the kind evident in the capital. Ending in two volutes linked by a small triangle, the capital descends from the Egyptian lily shape and is one of the precursors of the Ionic capital in Greece. Not intended to bear loads, but to be a pleasing transitional feature between beam and pillar, its character is decidedly elegant, and its modelling and linear curves are fluent.

It is significant for more than the identification of this building that the seal of one Shema ebed Jeroboam was found in one of its rooms (fig. 28). The seal belonged to a minister of Jeroboam II, for the word 'ebed', like our 'minister', means servant and describes the same rank. It also confirms Amos's description of the luxury of the royal court. It is a delicate masterpiece of intaglio work, made of jasper, with the symbol of a very Babylonian roaring lion carved into it. The way the lion and his lashing tail curve into the oval, while the inscription of the seal fills in the background, makes it a masterpiece of small-scale sculpture, a rare but significant remnant of personal culture. A second seal was found nearby, belonging to one Asaph, an oval lapis lazuli with a symbol showing a demonic hybrid creature, a winged lion with a human torso and the crowned head of the royal Egyptian sparrowhawk (fig. 29). The same symbol, with the creature couchant, occurs on the seal of a man called Hosea, made of green jasper, now in the British Museum. It is significant that Shema's seal also has a companion piece, a seal belonging to the same official and found in Jerusalem.

The interesting point, and one which justifies us in viewing this period as marking the zenith of Israelite seal design, is that we also have two equally important seals belonging to officials serving King Uzziah, who ruled the kingdom of Judah at the same time. Uzziah must have been a remarkable character: he conquered the Philistines, made himself master of the land east of the Jordan, and acquired a port on the Red Sea. He fortified Jerusalem, organized the army, and grew so proud that he assumed the office of priest in the temple himself. His minister had a seal expressing considerable pride: it is double-sided, but while one side simply bears the name and office of Shebanya ebed Uzziah placed between two winged solar disks, the other shows a standing man in a long garment with an Egyptian sceptre in his left hand, his right hand held up in command and the inscription 'Shebanya', which tells us that this is to be taken as a portrait – and so far as I am aware the only occurrence of a personal portrait on a seal in the generally impersonal art of this early period. Another minister of Uzziah, called Abijah, was much more modest; his seal, besides bearing his name, shows a small Egyptian figure of a god which is also found on the crystal seal of one Assijah the son of Joachim. The figurative symbols are not really surprising in the context of a basically irreligious section of society. Once, and only once, the seal of a man with a Hebrew name shows a bearded divinity enthroned between symbolic palms. This has been explained as a picture of the god of Israel, an interpretation which is certainly as incorrect as if the little Egyptian god had been thus honoured. The lion on the seal from Megiddo, the ox on the seal of one Shamaiah, son of Azariah, can appear as symbols of divine power like the cherub in the temple, and in the utterances of the prophets as mere allegory, a kind of pictorial language designed for emotional effect. The dish-like palmette or stylized, curtailed palm tree on the seal of a man called Chananiah ben Akbor also belong to the same style of art as that of the temple. The fact that undoubted images

57

of gods occur on some seals proves that the Biblical account of the adoption of heathen cults in Israel is correct.

Building with stone pillars, as found in this period, became the accepted style throughout the later period of the Kings. In Megiddo, probably at the same time as the larger palace was built, a building of dressed stone was constructed on the east wall. It had a number of small rooms and one larger one, its roof was supported on stone bearers, and it was probably a storehouse; the rooms are all rectangular and strikingly narrow. The whole complex may have been linked to a city gate. Later, it was replaced by a very impressive structure containing large rooms. The stone pillars are always free-standing bearers, carrying canopies in the courtyard rooms, and in a rather later building in Megiddo they may even have surrounded three sides of a courtyard supporting a roof designed to give shade, a precursor of the Hellenic peristyle. Stone had now replaced wood everywhere as a building material. In the same way as stone pillars were the cornerstones of the palace in Megiddo, a whole wall has been found in Taanach built of brick, with stones inserted at regular intervals as reinforcement: a kind of stone half-timbering.

It was particularly unfortunate for these pillared buildings that archaeologists set about their excavations in Palestine with so many preconceived theological ideas. At first none of the stone pillars were recognized as architectural, and were taken for standing stones. They seemed more important than what lay around them, and as a result almost as much was destroyed as was excavated. With it went the chance of understanding it later. The wall in Taanach was simply torn down, and as there happened to be ten of the pillars, not natural rock formations but dressed stone, they were explained as being monuments to the tribes of Israel. Similarly, pillars which had been parts of oil presses were regarded as sanctuaries. The worst of it was that all this confused the dating. Such ideas suggested connections to the researchers and obscured the actual findings. Archaeologists were usually very unwilling to bring themselves to assign the pillars to any but the Canaanite period, since they were not in keeping with Israelite religion. Consequently what is certainly a deposit of late Jewish ceramics in Ain Shems was identified as Canaanite, and the

FIG. 30 Pottery vessels from the time of the Kings.
In the possession of Frau Emmy Roth, Berlin.

dating of ceramic development was greatly confused.

We know much more about it now, for the finds of pottery in particular are remarkably rich (fig. 30). Many of them have been found in the ruins of houses, particularly in Jericho, and in tombs. Like the other peoples of antiquity, Israel buried food and household utensils in the grave with its dead, lavishing care on the deceased's continued material existence in the next world. From ancient times onwards burials were often in caves. We frequently find a stone bench left in a kind of anteroom, probably a requisite of the funeral meal, and there is always a lamp. Originally intended to light the dead person in the darkness of the next world, it gradually took on deep symbolical meaning as ideas about that next world became less material. All kinds of vessels for every imaginable purpose have also been found: ewers and dishes, jugs and bottles. A characteristic utensil is a broad dish on a tall stem. Unlike the Canaanite pots, the later ceramics seem more massive in both design and material, broader and heavier. But in any case the influx of imported goods had slowed down, and the shapes were more Israelite. A consequence of urban culture was to make it necessary to manufacture ceramics efficiently.

Surprisingly, decorated utensils from the time of the Kings are very

FIG. 31 (*left*) Painted incense burner from Megiddo.
FIG. 32 (*right*) Clay stove from Taanach.

rare. We have only two major pieces, although they are very interesting and show how deeply the royal culture had permeated the people. One is a limestone incense burner found in Megiddo (fig. 31). Originally, as a similar piece shows, it was about 60 cm high, and stood on a stem-like foot surrounded by drooping leaves. The dish is an open shape surrounded by a garland of closed and open lotus flowers. The way the shape of the vessel becomes the shape of a plant, like the calyx motif itself, is Egyptian; one thinks of Egyptian pillars.

The second item is a pottery object 90 cm in height, with four walls and squared fire-holes, obviously an oven of some kind (fig. 32). Sellin found it in Taanach, along with a second piece of the same kind but unfortunately in very poor condition. It is symmetrically decorated with crude relief sculptures. The ornamentation is exclusively figurative. The front shows two ibexes on their hind legs beside a tree – a motif now known to have existed in very ancient Babylon and very ancient Egypt, although the mythological meaning it certainly had is entirely obscure to us. On each of the side walls, heads jutting towards the front wall and thus framing it, are three winged figures with sturdy animal bodies and human heads; between them are two lions, their front paws propped on their heads, and the left wall at the side shows a boy strangling a snake. A confused assembly of fabulous creatures has thus been shown on the item, in a very perfunctorily arrangement, and although they correspond to the cherubim of the decoration of the temple and must be derived from them, they seem far coarser than the description of Huram-abi's work in the temple. The item shows a kind of folk art developing in Israel, a broader adaptation of features imported into the country by Solomon's artists.

It did not have time to develop fully. Despite all the alliances that had been concluded, and with nothing to weaken it from within, the northern kingdom was conquered in 720 BCE by the Assyrians, who were now much more powerful, and its people were taken into exile. This was nothing but the defeat of a small nation by a much larger one, but the event is unique in history because it did not put an end to Israel's spiritual mission. The reason may be that initially the southern kingdom remained unaffected, and as a result its religious centre, Jerusalem, became the spiritual centre and focal point for Israel as a whole: only now did the Jewish religion really begin to show all its profundity and spirituality. The time of King Josiah may be described as the period when it actually confessed its faith, and the year 621, when the king proclaimed the authority of the 'book of the law' in the temple as its first really clear moment of definition. This was when the horses and chariots of the sun god and the figure of Astarte in the temple itself were destroyed, an event which says much in itself. The many local cultic sites, including the ancient one of Bethel in the northern kingdom, were destroyed at this time. All the demands of the prophets, the people's religious leaders, had now been fulfilled. When the southern kingdom itself was conquered by Babylon in 586, and Solomon's temple and palace were burnt, while the temple implements were looted and a terrible punishment was visited on what remained of the people of Judah, who went into exile, the temple itself remained so much their spiritual centre as a religious concept that it continued to exist in the hearts of the nation, and religious unity, identical with national unity, was secured in spite of political disaster.

CHAPTER THREE

Israel among the Peoples of Antiquity

AND NOW a tragedy unparalleled in history begins. The two king
doms of Israel had been defeated, their land conquered, a large
part of the people taken away to foreign countries and settled
among strangers – yet they did not forget their home and their freedom.
The consciousness of being *one* people, owing allegiance to *one* religion,
was one they maintained with determination. Israel clung to the idea of
its temple, its land and its teachings. The historical awareness of belonging
together remained alive in circumstances in which any nation with less
of a sense of tradition would have lost it.

The aim of the people was always to regain their own country and
their temple in Jerusalem. Israel fought for it with a tenacity, a power of
self-sacrifice, an expense of courage and patience, and of active and passive
energy, that only the greatest faith can engender. And when hope was
finally gone, when Jerusalem and the temple were lost for ever after Bar
Kochba's last battle, the Jewish philosophy of life was born amidst endless
spiritual struggles within the nation: struggles between mystics and
rationalists, orthodox and assimilated Jews, schools of thought and
doctrinal opinions. The awareness of being a Jew became a spiritual
home, replacing the land and worship in the temple. We have to imagine
the environment in which these people lived to appreciate the sheer size
of their mental achievement. It was the period of Hellenism, as classical
antiquity drew to a close under Roman rule. Culture was now international,
with trade roads and shipping routes linking all the countries around the
Mediterranean. Harbours such as Alexandria, or markets such as Palmyra
and Antioch, took everything the outlying countries could produce and

conveyed it on its way. There was no nationalist feeling in this world until the second century, when Germanic and Slavonic peoples began migrating into Europe. Where any such feeling was in fact present, among the Germanic and Gaulish tribes and among the Jews, it was savagely suppressed. The wars of Julius Caesar and Titus are two acts of the same tragedy. Yet although the Jews were dispersed throughout the world of the time, they still retained their sense of communal identity.

Spiritually, there was even more to contend with. The Greek and Roman religions, initially as fundamentally different as the peoples of Hellas and Italy themselves, had merged into a very vague imperial religion which had absorbed a great deal of philosophy. In between mysticism and materialism a medley of religious and philosophical views existed, the vague and improbable notions of dozens of religions and systems. From Persia to Gaul, the most daring of mystery cults were taught side by side with each other and indiscriminately believed. The Persian god Mithras and the Egyptian goddess Isis, Baal and Cybele, Orpheus and Dionysos, ruled the same cities and the same minds. On the surface, this state of affairs meant some relief for Judaism: there was nothing to prevent it continuing to exist in any country. Beneath the surface, however, it took an extraordinary amount of energy not to be simply submerged in the mystical whirlpool and become just one of the many Oriental religions. The extremely logical and precise Jewish mind, however, was well aware that all these cults were less credible than its own religion and could lay less claim to the truth than its clear-cut monotheism. As critical a mind as that of Lucian, who was a Syrian and must have been close to the Jews of his time, in his faculty of judgement at least, not only rejects contemporary beliefs and philosophical systems but regards them with distinct irony. He obviously despised them. Jewry was thus strengthened in its conviction of being a special and even rather superior case among other peoples.

At first it had seemed as if the wishes of the exiles would soon be granted. Barely forty years after the first destruction of the temple, the Persians under Cyrus (559–529 BCE) made themselves masters of Asia. They conquered Babylon, subdued all its domains and even vanquished Egypt. Palestine too fell into their hands. There may have been deeper reasons for the Achaemenid kings to feel kindly disposed to their Jewish subjects: the Persian religion was not in effect idol-worship, but strongly emphasized ethics. Its two divinities Ormuzd and Ahriman personified the opposition between good and evil, light and darkness. They are not so much gods in the heathen sense as the manifestations of a moral system of world government. One gets the impression that this philosophy made the Persians tolerant of the Jews, letting them feel that their religions were related. At any rate, Jews played a certain part at court close to the king. In the year 536 Cyrus gave permission for them to return to their land and build a temple, and returned from his treasury the gold and silver utensils plundered from the first temple. Building began with the altar, and worship with the offering of sacrifices. However, at the same time there were problems arising from the presence of the mixed population that had now settled in Palestine and did not want to have to contest its rights. Another and uncompromising decree from the Persian king Darius was necessary before the second temple under Joshua and Zerubbabel could be considered finished. A renaissance of Judaism came only with Ezra and Nehemiah, who fortified Jerusalem again in the middle of the fifth century to enable the city to defend itself.

The second temple did not compare with the first in size and splendour. It was more of a religious centre than a work of architecture, and was built in great haste to a simple plan. The crucial point was to have a house of God; artistic values did not matter. The accounts in the book of Ezra, accordingly, are very brief, telling us only that 'the height thereof was threescore cubits, and the breadth thereof threescore cubits'. It probably consisted only of the two main parts, the *hekal* and *debir*. The walls were said to be three rows of stones thick, and encased in timber. The building certainly had no gold leaf or other ornamentation at first. It is difficult to say for sure whether the seven-branched candlestick beside which the prophet Zechariah saw Joshua and Zerubbabel standing, in the form of two olive trees, was anything more than a vision, but it probably was. In any case, the passage is very important for the history of Jewish symbolism. However, the books of Ezra and Nehemiah, which are generally very accurate, explicitly mention only the vessels of the first temple which had been looted by the Persians and which they later returned. These were not of course the vessels of Solomon's temple, stolen long ago by Shishak, but were made by later kings, and from the list given, which speaks only of dishes, basins and knives, they were by far less diverse and interesting. No mention is made of candlesticks, and the ark of the covenant, the focal point of the people's religion, was absent from the holy of holies in the second temple. One can understand why, as the Biblical account tells us, old men who had known the first temple wept.

After Israel's return to its own country it would have been possible for a Jewish culture to come into being. The beginnings of such a thing were present and beginning to develop. However, the land did not have peace, for its overlords kept changing over the next few centuries, each making different demands and exacting their fulfilment from the people who were their subjects. Alexander the Great took Palestine along with the Persian empire in 331. His military commanders, who divided up his vast empire among themselves after his death, could not agree, and the dynasties they founded continued quarrelling over its various parts. Palestine's historical misfortune in being a bone of contention between its Asiatic and Egyptian neighbours meant that it first went to the Syrian Seleucus, then, in 301, to the Ptolemies who were rulers of Egypt, and then again to the Syrians in 198. While the highly cultivated Ptolemies, especially Ptolemy Philadelphus who had the Bible translated into Greek and gave the temple valuable utensils, took an objective view of their Jewish subjects, the Syrians savagely persecuted the Jewish religion. Finally there were the persecutions of Antiochus Epiphanes, who had an image of Jupiter set up in the temple itself, ordered the sacrifice of pigs, and inflicted terrible punishment on those who held to their faith. This was intolerable to Jewish piety and pride. The nation's will to resist and fight for its freedom grew more strongly than ever before. The result was the heroic rising of the Maccabees. Judas Maccabeus conquered Jerusalem, and worship in the temple began again in 164. After the death of Judas his brothers Jonathan and Simon, constantly engaged in hard fighting, forced a recognition of independence from the Syrians. Simon, and in the next generation his son John Hyrcanus, were kings and high priests at the same time – an important recognition of the identity of religion and nation in Israel. They were the independent rulers of a people that had won its freedom.

This period is of particular interest in the history of art. It saw the infiltration of Greek art into the east, which was increasingly subject to its influence. That influence made its way as far as India. Alexander the Great opened the way to it, and his successors smoothed its path, founding cities that were like so many nurseries of Greek art all over Asia. However, all these countries had had their own art for centuries. Their inhabitants had religions of their own, requirements of their own, and above all they had a great deal of imagination. Consequently, the east did not simply adopt Greek art: the cool clarity of Greece absorbed the wealth of forms that the Orient already possessed. The result was the rich style known as Hellenistic, a style of unbridled fantasy, perhaps the freest artistic style in history. In architecture and crafts alike, ornamentation prevailed over structural logic in a wonderful mingling of eastern and western forms. In Alexandria, the realism that had always been the creative element in Egyptian art overcame the cool classicism of Hellenic sculpture and painting.

The Orient as a whole, then, did not simply become subject to Hellenism but absorbed and re-created it. In Palestine, however, even that did not happen. To Jews, the Greek spirit was merely paganism, and they opposed Greek art as determinedly as they opposed the Greek religion. They did not entirely escape Greek influence, particularly in colloquial speech, which unconsciously absorbed many Greek words, especially for new institutions: even the Talmud is full of them. Such generally familiar words as 'synhedrion' and 'synagogue' are Greek. However, the depiction of figures and images was probably never so strictly avoided in Jewish art as during the Hellenistic period. For Jews, the period did not favour artistic activities anyway. Who was going to commission works of art and create them amidst such insecurity? The temple was poorer than ever, the heads of state and religious leaders had plenty to do in defending what they had. The most important artistic achievement known to us is on a very small scale, consisting of the Maccabean coinage.

It was natural for coins to be minted, since now that the state was free again one of its first tasks must be to demonstrate its sovereignty in its own currency and its own coins. The stamps on these coins are of great interest in the history of Jewish art because they show, for the first time, the tendency towards symbolism which was to remain part of Jewish art thereafter.

Symbolism in itself is not much more than picture-writing. It is the most abstract means of representing an object, depicted not as itself but as an allusion to an idea. The aim is clarity rather than sensuous form. The idea incarnated in the Maccabean symbols on the coinage is the idea of Jewry. They show the vessels used in divine service, the wine-cup and the branches of the 'four species' of foliage for the feast of Tabernacles (the seven-branched candelabrum, which was the dominant symbol only a short time later, is still entirely absent), as well as the produce of the country: ears of corn, the fig leaf, the bunch of grapes, and above all the palm tree, the symbol of Judah. Alexander Yannai, who won access to the sea – a significant event at a time when exchanging goods was as important as producing them – stamped an anchor on his coins. No human images appear on the Maccabean coins, but the Herods diverge from custom in this respect as well as others, adopting the Roman type of coinage. With Agrippa II, the ruler's portrait and even the classical goddess of victory feature. It was natural for Bar Kochba to return immediately to a design for the coinage without any such images.

Greek influence made itself felt stylistically throughout the period. It may sound paradoxical that as a consequence what little Maccabean art we have, despite its strict avoidance of all Greek subjects and ideas, still looks very Greek. However, Hellenism had become the style of the period, was entirely international, and made its way unconsciously and unnoticed into all the art forms of all lands. The very fact that everything created by the Jewish people was created solely to fulfil a purpose, and was not intended as a work of art, inevitably made it subject to a style whose own national characteristics had become so diluted that no one noticed them.

A Palestinian town of the period, accordingly, looked like a Hellenistic

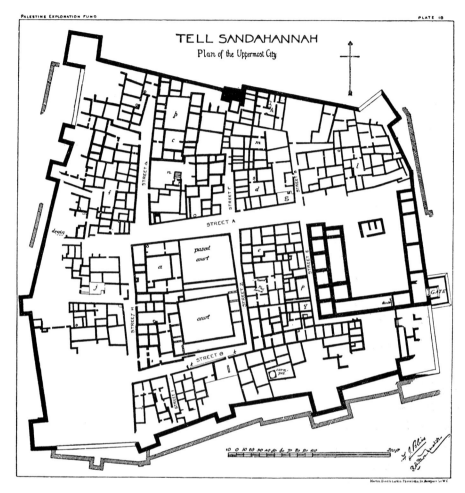

FIG. 33 Plan of the city of Mareshah.

town on a small scale. Excavations have uncovered the ground plan of Mareshah during the Seleucid period (fig. 33), a town fiercely disputed in the conflicts fought by Judas Maccabeus and John Hyrcanus. We no longer find houses clustering within the city walls like the cells of a honeycomb, as in the past. Deliberate planning is obvious everywhere. All the ground plans have been drawn with a straight rule and a square. The city wall, a strong double structure, no longer follows the curve of the hill but faces four ways, to all points of the compass, and is reinforced by square towers. These towers, and indeed the whole of the rest of the town, were built

FIG. 34 Castle of John Hyrcanus, completed ground plan.

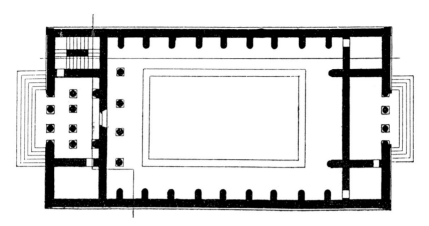

FIG. 35 Castle of John Hyrcanus, part of the east wall.

of limestone blocks. The design is dominated by roads to carry traffic. A broad paved street bisects the town from east to west, with side streets running off it at right angles. The richest houses are situated in the middle of the town, built round paved courtyards, while cramped rooms are clustered close together in the poorer quarters. The largest building, obviously a public one, is just behind the city gate on the east side. This corresponds to Palestinian custom: in ancient times the citizens always assembled by the gate, where a town full of nooks and crannies was likely to have most open space, and where incoming traffic would bring news. The existence of a special gatehouse is in accordance with the new method of building to a plan. The courtyard is the most important part of it: the buildings are relatively narrow structures around the sides. If, as we may assume, the townspeople met for worship, it must have been here. However, the building cannot be called a synagogue at this date; it would simply have been used like one. The courtyard also probably acted as a market place: not only did everything coming in through the gate have to pass this way, but it was situated where the main street began. The design of this courtyard, then, was very much like the *agora* of Greek towns, except that it was not in the middle of the town (as in Priene, for instance) but near the gate. Again, Greek building has been adapted to the custom of the country in a manner typical of Hellenism in Palestine and one which encouraged national pride.

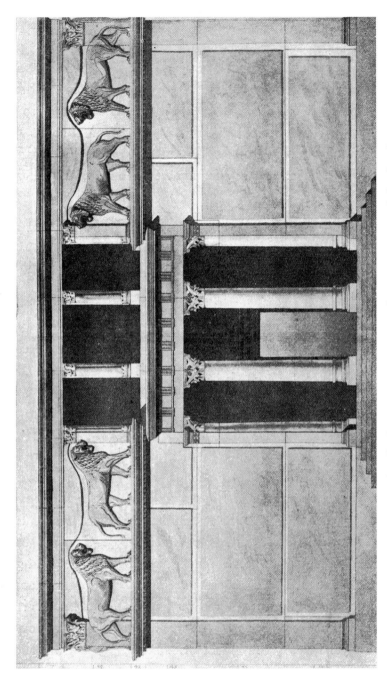

Fig. 36 Castle of John Hyrcanus, attempted reconstruction of the façade.

This also explains why the one building of some size we still have, built by one of the Maccabean princes, displays so many distinctly Greek features. Josephus describes it in such detail that we can still recognize its remains today. He tells us that John Hyrcanus the Tobid (135–105) built a large complex east of the Jordan, between Arabia and Judaea, and called it Tyrus. The main building, surrounded by a defensive moat, was entirely made of white stone and surrounded by a relief of gigantic animal figures. An extensive complex of caves was made ready in the rocks of the mountain range opposite, obviously as a secure refuge.

All this, including the situation, exactly fits Arak il Emir in East Jordan. The main building, the Kasr il Abd, frequently mentioned in Bedouin legends, must be John Hyrcanus's castle. It was laid out in a rectangle around a courtyard (fig. 34). The narrower walls, which had entrances in them, were about 20 metres long, and the longer walls about 40 metres long. Part of the eastern wall is still standing, and shows where the animal frieze stood, marked off from the main wall of large dressed stones by a narrow Greek denticulation (fig. 35), although the animals themselves were hacked away at a later date, in the same period of strict orthodoxy which, on religious grounds, destroyed the animals ornamenting early Palestinian synagogues. Most of the creatures here were probably striding lions. The gates on the narrow sides were pillared (fig. 36) and gave access to a courtyard surrounded by pillared porticos. The living quarters were on several storeys around the courtyard.

Native and foreign forms thus combined in this building to form a curious but charming hybrid. The layout round a pillared courtyard, a peristyle, is undoubtedly Oriental. So is the animal frieze, whose history can be traced back to the friezes on Phoenician bowls by way of the Ishtar Gate built by Nebuchadnezar in Babylon. All the other structures, in particular the capitals of the pillars, are Corinthian, the richest of the Greek styles. The two splendid gates in the encircling wall were also very much in the Greek manner. One of them even bore an eagle, the image that so horrified the people on Herod's temple. Obviously the sacrilege lay not in its being made at all, only in placing it on the house of the Lord. Josephus comments, in this connection, that the law forbids any

FIG. 37 The temple of Herod and the Antonia Mount,
attempted reconstruction by M. de Vogué.

idea of setting up graven images and consecrating the likenesses of
animals. It is obvious, then, that the presence of the eagle on a *secular*
building, such as John Hyrcanus's, was not regarded as sinful, but on
Herod's temple it was.

None the less, the artistic difference between the two buildings is
remarkably large. Herod (37–4 BCE), an Idumaean, was a Hellenic prince
like all other such princes in Asia. He wanted his buildings to display his
splendour. What John Hyrcanus ventured to do only once, and that very
hesitantly, came perfectly naturally to Herod. He built himself a
magnificent palace in his capital city, Jerusalem, erected a theatre in the
Greek style for the performance of plays, and an amphitheatre for wild
beast baiting and gladiatorial games – two types of buildings with no
roots at all in Palestine, merely intended, like the spectacles staged in
them, to present a dazzling picture of Herod's royal power. He rebuilt
the temple not out of a sense of religious duty but so that the principal
sanctuary of his land should not lag behind those of neighbouring
countries.

FIG. 38 The triumphal procession of Titus,
relief on the Arch of Titus in Rome.

Josephus's descriptions and occasional remarks in the Mishnah provide quite a clear picture of the temple in its final form (fig. 37). Its furnishings were now largely devoted not so much to worship as to religious purification. This building again shows how, in the development of the Jewish religion, the emphasis had shifted increasingly to the spiritual element. The question of who was worthy to enter which part of the sanctuary occupied the minds of teachers as much as the ritual of sacrifice, or even more. The circle of those allowed access grew narrower and narrower from the periphery of the city of Jerusalem, in itself a holy place, to the innermost holy of holies. The vessels required for purification stood in many parts of the temple precinct. It has been calculated that on the Day of Atonement the high priest had to take no less than five full baths, as well as washing his hands and feet ten times, and every visitor to the temple had to enter it in a state of religious purity for which the stipulations were very strict.

The whole layout of the temple, then, was determined by religious requirements. It was obviously planned as a combination of the descriptions of the tabernacle and of Solomon's temple. This intention accounts for its large spatial extent. The temple itself lay in the innermost of three courtyards: the outer courtyard, coinciding with the extent of the plateau of the mount itself, the second, which women might enter, and the third, to which only priests had access, with the exception of a narrow area left for the people. Behind the great altar of sacrifice in this courtyard rose a vast wall, 100 cubits both tall and broad, and the door in it, 40 cubits high and 20 cubits broad, measured exactly the same as the innermost temple itself. This lay behind a broad vestibule 20 cubits broad, 40 cubits high and 60 cubits long, which contained two rooms, the *hekal*, measuring 40 cubits in length, and the holy of holies, which was 20 cubits long. The upper storey was divided in the same way. This was the layout sanctified in Solomon's temple, but the beautiful proportions then created voluntarily were now deliberately copied, and as with every copy, the effect must have seemed rather calculated. Above all, the building's towering height must have made it seem massive rather than beautiful. On religious grounds, the figurative ornamentation of the building was more restrained than was usual in the Hellenistic and Roman east. None the less, it did include the great golden eagle to which the devout took such exception. There is also mention of a precious golden vine running all around the frame of the curtained portal allowing access to the inner temple, a decorative motif which, carved in stone, surrounds the frames of many Syrian gateways of the time. The interior of the temple building was lined with gold, all the building materials were very expensive, and the curtains were masterpieces of the weaver's art. We know nothing much from the written accounts about the appearance of the temple utensils, but we do have a good depiction of certain items in the relief on the Arch of Titus (fig. 38). This is the most important pictorial evidence in ancient Jewish history, for these must have been the vessels of the temple taken to Rome by Titus when Jerusalem finally fell, and displayed in the city streets at his triumph.

The relief shows the unadorned table for the showbread being carried in front (fig. 40). On it stand two cups, deep goblets without a stem. They are plain in shape, simpler than the cups on the Maccabean coinage. The

FIGS 39 & 40 The temple utensils on the Arch of Titus.

slender temple trumpets carried crossing each other in front of the table are absolutely plain too. Then, and for the first time, comes the seven-branched candelabrum or menorah (fig. 39). It is particularly fortunate that the menorah is shown, since it subsequently became the principal symbol throughout the history of Jewish art.

The Arch of Titus clearly shows the menorah in two artistically incongruous parts. The actual candlesticks consist of six branches and the central trunk from which they symmetrically proceed. The small lamps they supported are not visible. The lower part of the central trunk is thickened to form a kind of base. With its drooping leaves, it resembles the bases of Persian pillars in Susa and Persepolis. The shape of the branches and the pattern of alternation between curved and flat sections is Oriental too; it occurred as early as the Hittites and then spread all over the east. The candelabrum itself stands on a hexagonal or more likely octagonal plinth. There are tritons on its sides, and in general it looks extremely Roman. This is where the problem becomes very difficult. The depiction of the upper part of the candelabrum must be accurate; it corresponds in its essentials to the details of the seven-branched

FIG. 41 Ruins of the basilica on the site of excavations, Samaria.
The remains of the niche are in the foreground.

candlestick of the tabernacle, and thus fits the symbolism which ruled
the temple and its courtyards. But whose work was it, and how did it
come to be mounted on a Graeco-Roman plinth? The equipment of
Zerubbabel's temple, which may have included a seven-branched
candelabrum, had been removed by Antiochus and replaced by Judas
Maccabeus. If he had imitated the seven-branched candlestick of
Zerubbabel, we would have expected it to stand on a base of a Persian
type. Unlikely as it is that Herod had all the equipment newly made, it
would have been like him to place the sacred shape of the upper part on
a heathen base, thus modernizing it. We may credit the man who had the
eagle set above the temple door with the tritons on the base of the
candelabrum as well.

Outside Jerusalem, Herod was subject to far fewer constraints in his
artistic endeavours. Caesarea, which he built as a harbour town on the
Mediterranean, seems from Josephus's description to have been a kind of
miniature Alexandria, with its palace, warehouses, halls, houses and
promenades. It was regarded as a brilliant model, and its influence in
Judaea became more and more perceptible with the passage of time. We

78

know of several old cities rebuilt with great splendour by Herod, and the excavations of Samaria provide us with the best idea of them today.

Samaria was fortified too, of course, to shore up Herod's rule, and the defensive wall, 3.25 metres thick, was reinforced by strong round bastions. However, the layout of the complex as a whole was no longer functionally determined. The aim, instead, was for a large and impressive spatial effect. The Hellenistic town, as we saw in Mareshah, had straight streets with a clear view in one direction, thus creating the basis of the art of town planning which was fully developed in Roman times. The word 'Roman' here indicates only a period, not an artistic style, for the leading stylistic influence was eastern, and can be traced even in buildings of the same kind in Rome and Pompeii which tried to imitate the great palatial residences of the Orient. Samaria was a relatively modest place, for Judaea was a small country and Samaria was not even its capital city. Even here, however, there was a wide street lined with pillars going right through the town, an imposing design suggesting a festive processional way. This must certainly have been the main street, since the bazaars lay beside it. The market place or agora was also impressively designed and surrounded by a vaulted colonnade. It contained the basilica – the royal hall and seat of justice (fig. 41). Its paved court was surrounded in turn by a pillared hall, and the throne of judgement stood in a semi-circular niche opposite the entrance. At the top of the hill, visible from afar and magnificent in appearance, Herod built the temple of Caesar Augustus. This was an act of slavish humility to the emperor: here in Samaria he could venture to do something impossible in Jerusalem and allow the hated Roman imperial cult a place. The temple was a magnificent building with a mighty pillared portico, an ante-room and an inner cella, surrounded by pillars, where the image of the emperor stood. A badly mutilated imperial statue has been found in Samaria. Of course the city also had an amphitheatre in the Roman style.

After the catastrophe of the year 70, the conquest of Jerusalem, the destruction of the temple by Titus and the final devastation of the city under Hadrian in 135 CE, coinciding with the total loss of national independence, there were no external barriers left to hold back the advance

FIG. 42 The ruins of Gerasa, a view down the pillared street.

of heathen culture into Palestine. Artistically, the country was entirely Hellenized and became a province of the Graeco-Oriental style. Within its modest means, Palestine reproduced what can be seen on a larger scale in the ruins of Palmyra with its gigantic pillared street, its temples and arches, or in the remains of the temple to the gods in Baalbek. Jews were banned from Jerusalem in 135 CE. It became an entirely heathen city under the name of Aelia Capitolina, with temples to the gods and statues of them, and a picture of it on the mosaic of a fifth-century Palestinian church shows that its main artery was the typical pillared street. Amman in East Jordan, already Hellenized by the Ptolemies, acquired its magnificent buildings at this time. Petra, the chief city of the Nabateans and an important centre of trade between Arabia and Syria, took up the ancient type of stone sepulchre at the same period and gave it a new form. Its plain *trompe l'oeil* façades and house-like shape progressively developed into the magnificent illusion of a palace, with brilliant variants heightening the splendour of Hellenism and all the fantasy peculiar to the Orient in baroque contrasts. These tombs have façades showing two storeys, their basically classical forms interrupted with curious abruptness, and resumed just as abruptly for no apparent reason.

The most interesting site in Palestine is the ruined Roman city of Gerasa (fig. 42). There are still so many buildings of the Roman period standing here that we can get a good idea of the entire layout. The typical pillar-lined street ran straight through the town from a semi-circular area also surrounded by pillars, near one of the two theatres. The porticos of the street provided shade. Arches rose above the street crossings. A large temple of Artemis, a sanctuary of the nymphs, and the large baths found in every town of classical antiquity, are arranged so as to make the city appear an impressive unit. Again, of course there was a city wall.

However, this was also the period when the Jewish congregation and Jewish prayer began taking shape, and when scholars were expanding the doctrine and ethics of Judaism. The temple of Jerusalem and sacrificial worship in it might be gone, but now communities found their centres in the synagogue and in prayer. In fact the Diaspora itself had an extraordinarily stimulating effect on creative art. It sounds almost blasphemous to say that only the Diaspora made Jewish art possible, yet it is literally true. For while the national temple presented a major architectural task only two or three times, and its stock of vessels and ornaments was relatively small, there were now many more occasions for artistic achievement. Jewish communities existed throughout the inhabited world, from Spain to India. Many of them were of great importance, and many were extremely prosperous. Their expenditure on divine worship was correspondingly large. Schools and synagogues (the two were initially synonymous), burial vaults, sacred utensils and books were all needed, and the decorative art in which this period rejoiced did not stop short at items connected with Jewish worship. They too were adorned and became works of art, like those of all other religions; people ornamented them because they treasured them. Strict as the limitations imposed by custom and the Law might be, this was artistically the most valuable period in the entire course of Jewish history. The Jews were no longer living as a free nation in their own country, yet they were free citizens of foreign cities and lived within the cultural context of their surroundings. Hatred and persecution of Jews had been rife since the beginning of the Roman period, but still absent was the inhumane ostracism and contempt shown to them in the Christian Middle Ages, which stifled not only outer freedom but that inner freedom which alone makes art possible. In addition, a strong desire for self-assertion determined Jewish attitudes at this time. Religion and doctrine had taken the place of the temple, and the Jews were energetically constructing their own world of ideas and feelings. These two factors, their own activity and the intellectual activity of their environment, combined into a display of genuine creative power. A student coming to the history of Jewish art for the first time at the watershed between classical antiquity and the Middle Ages will be almost alarmed by the wealth of buildings and other works of art from this period, and the significance of the questions they raise, which are of importance for more than merely Jewish art. The body of works is so extensive that it will be necessary to discuss each country concerned separately.

First, the homeland of Palestine. It retained religious hegemony in the first centuries after the destruction of Jerusalem; its patriarchs and religious authorities were the recognized leaders of the whole world of Jewry. There were outward and visible signs of that fact. In the cities of Palestine, particularly in Galilee, which led the way, the synagogues were undoubtedly the most important buildings of the imperial Roman period. Their ruins are the only significant remains of antiquity in these towns; they were built of solid stone that has survived the centuries. We have the ruins of at least forty synagogues, twelve of which in Galilee alone and a number of others throughout the country have been closely studied. They were so significant, and their ornamentation so lavish, that they provide a real picture of the life of the Jewish communities of Palestine at the time of the compilation of the Talmud. They were not in a state of stultification or gloom. Even after the destruction of the temple there was a flourishing Jewish society in Palestine, and one not without its own lustre.

FIG. 43 The façade of the synagogue of Kefr Birim.

FIG. 44 Ruins of the façade of the synagogue of Meron.

FIG. 45 (*left*) The synagogue of Tell Hum (Capernaum), keystone of an arch.

FIG. 46 (*right*) The synagogue in Tell Hum (Capernaum), console of the main portal.

One of the most beautiful of the Palestinian synagogues was in Tell Hum, formerly Capernaum, standing on a high terrace with a fine view of the Sea of Tiberias; there were others in Chorazin, Irbid (Arbela), Meron, two in Giskala and two in Kefr Birim. Outside Galilee, there are important remains of synagogues in Ashdod, Silo, Naaran, and what is now the modern settlement of Beth Alpha. Tradition has recorded the existence of many others, such as those of Sepphoris and the thirteen synagogues in Tiberias, towns which were two of the principal seats of Jewish scholarship. The dimensions of these buildings were considerable. In only some of the buildings was he frontal length less than fifteen metres, and it usually approached twenty metres. In addition there were subsidiary buildings, making the synagogue a very impressive complex, a genuine centre of community life. In line with the taste of the period the narrower side was usually, if not always, extended to form an impressive façade (figs 43, 44). In all the larger buildings three portals led to the

FIG. 47 The central portal of the synagogue of Kefr Birim.

FIG. 48 Portal of the second synagogue of Kefr Birim (no longer extant).

interior, a tall portal flanked by two smaller ones. They were richly decorated, and the coping in particular, which projected some way to the side above the supporting pillars and often rested on consoles, bore a wealth of relief ornamentation showing animals, garlands and symbols (figs 45, 46). In one case, in Kefr Birim, parts of a vestibule with pillars have been preserved, and the richly decorated portals would have come

FIG. 49 The synagogue of Irbid, reconstruction of the interior.

into view only behind it. This vestibule, however, is so common a feature in the area that it will have been part of many of the synagogue buildings, at least the richer of them. Unfortunately, we know very little about the appearance of the façades as a whole, since only the lower parts to about the height of the portals are usually still standing; everything else lies on the ground in heaps of rubble and can be only fragmentarily reconstructed. However, we can be certain that the whole front was designed on a lavish scale, with an arched window over the central portal (fig. 47), windows with ornamented lintels at the sides, and a richly decorated pediment standing out sharply against the bright blue of the Palestinian sky. Each of these features had bands bearing lavish friezes of the classical Greek kind, with elements such as rows of leaves, palmettes, denticulations and beading, at this late period arbitrarily combined to create an even more magnificent effect (fig. 48).

As far as we know the interiors of all the Palestinian synagogues were

FIG. 50 The synagogue in Tell Hum (Capernaum), part of a cornice.

FIG. 51 The synagogue in Tell Hum (Capernaum), part of the wall frieze.

FIG. 52 The synagogue in Chorazin (Keraze), part of the frieze.

on the same pattern. This consisted of a rectangular hall with rows of pillars along three sides, dividing off a kind of ambulatory or side nave, which contained stone seats arranged in terraces like those in a Greek theatre – the best way for a large number of worshippers to follow the service. Above it, supported by the pillars of the main nave, was a gallery with its ceiling also supported on pillars, divided from the central area by a wooden balustrade. This gallery would have been for the women. The area could be an oblong, as in Tell Hum and Meron, or almost square, as in Irbid (fig. 49) and Giskala.

The impression of the interior must have been even richer than that of the façade. There is a solemn air about the rows of pillars, one above the other, with their decorated capitals usually of the Corinthian order. In addition there were decorative friezes, particularly lavish in Tell Hum (figs 50, 51) and Chorazin (fig. 52). They seem to have been on the interior of the wall and to have formed part of the cornice projecting above the pillars. They are filled with ornamental forms, projecting under lavishly moulded cornices and bearing acanthus tendrils and symbols. In at least five synagogues – Kefr Kenna, Naaran near Jericho, Beth Alpha and Amman, but not in Galilee, which remained faithful to the letter of the law – there were rich and partly figurative mosaics on the floor.

It is very difficult to decide what the interiors looked like: we can form almost no idea of the furnishings, since they have left nothing but vestigial traces behind. The archaeological report on the excavations in Tell Hum assumes that there was a stone ark for the Torah by the wall with the entrance, where people coming in would initially have had their backs to it. In most cases the ark must have been a tall wooden closet, as shown in depictions of the time. The whole building faced Jerusalem, and in Galilee therefore faced north, so that the congregation at prayer was always looking towards the temple and worshipping before the sanctuary, at least in spirit.

There is only one building, in Capernaum, which shows evidence of a pillared courtyard with a direct side entrance to the synagogue. However, we may assume that other synagogues had such a court too, and it may have served as a summer synagogue, since such walks and open-air courts

FIG. 53 Fragment of a synagogue
chest from Ashdod.

are very popular in the east and were very suitable for many of the religious
observances of Israel. I myself have seen the courtyard of the very modern
synagogue in Samarkand adorned with plants and used for divine service.

In Jewish literature, the component parts of the synagogue bear Greek
names. The general type is described as a basilica and its special form as
a diplostoon, because of the double pillared hall. The Talmud itself uses
these words without any apparent revulsion: they are part of the current
language of the time. The style and form of the ornamentation were
Hellenistic, the natural style of the period. What is present is Greek without
exception; we can learn more from what is absent. Nothing at all from
the entire Hellenic mythological world is shown, there is nothing drawn
from its opulent sensuous world, no landscape, no realistic animal, none
of its religious symbols. All these things were heathen, idolatrous, un-
Jewish. Pillars, pilasters, capitals and friezes, arches and niches favour the
rich decoration of the mixed Corinthian style predominant everywhere
in this late period of antiquity. Garlands and wreaths are as popular in

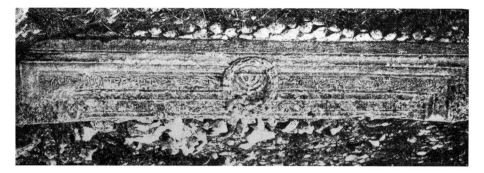

FIG. 54 Lintel of a door in the synagogue of En Nebraten.

FIG. 55 Lintel of a door in the synagogue of Siloh (Selun).

Palestine as in the rest of the Hellenized world. Among plant motifs, naturally, the stylized Corinthian acanthus predominates. The same applies to the animal kingdom. Animal figures in relief, most of them usually hacked away at a later period of stricter observance, were particularly common on the lavish ornamentation of the portals. They were usually eagles and lions, and even centaurs and Bacchic scenes appear in connection with the grape-vine, although never as realistically as in Greek reliefs. Such motifs were clearly adopted along with the ornamentation and felt to be nothing more.

To make a comparison: in the College for the Study of Judaism in Berlin the portal is flanked by two owls, the symbols of wisdom, and two cornucopias, the symbols of plenty, with the head of a lion in the middle. Two of these symbols are originally heathen: the owl as the bird of Minerva, and the cornucopia as the symbol of plenty given by the gods. The lion's head acts as an architectonic keystone. However, all this is so much part of the symbolism of our own time that we are no longer aware of its being at all heathen. It was the same with the decoration of the Palestinian synagogues. The Hellenistic style had become so universal, so generalized, that many typical elements were felt to be simply decorative. The interest is in noting what was rejected because it *was* felt to be heathen, and what was added because it was a Jewish symbol. Accordingly, we find the symbolic plants that had previously appeared on the Maccabean coinage, the vine and grapes in many different variants, and the palm tree. In addition, and this is a new feature, the cultic symbols appear, in particular the seven-branched candelabrum or menorah, which from now on became the chief symbol and marked every place where Jewry had a home in the ancient world. Why exactly it should have become the chief symbol is as much of a mystery as the modern significance of the six-pointed star of David. The reason must be in the mysticism of the time, for in the book of the prophet Zechariah the menorah is the central feature of a vision with the character of a mystic revelation of the fate of the world, a true apocalypse. However, none of the mystic literature of the Diaspora, unlike that of the Talmud, has been preserved. Yet surely, as the Jews of the time confronted their own destiny, this was the beginning of the opposition between rationalism and mysticism which was to be Israel's intellectual fate through all the centuries of exile. The mystic literature is the only likely source of the symbolism that first appears in the synagogues of Palestine. The seven-branched candelabrum occurs three times. Its shape as shown on a chest in a synagogue in Ashdod (fig. 53) is similar to that of the candelabrum on the Arch of Titus, with the symbolic foliage and the shofar horn beside it. On the other hand, a different shape occurs in Galilee on the lintel of the door in the synagogue of En Nebraten (fig. 54), and on a relief from Tiberias now in the Louvre in Paris. Here the menorah is shown quite plain and unadorned, as it was often depicted in the Jewish east later. A crosspiece links the tops of the seven branches, indicating that it was a small trough in which the seven little lamps were placed. A large amphora-like vessel appears several times (fig. 55), notably on a chest from the synagogue in Siloh, and there is a representation of the double-doored ark containing the scrolls of the Torah on a lintel in Tell Hum. Most of the symbols typical of the time, symbols repeatedly encountered from now on, were thus already known in sculpture. However, there is a very mysterious motif found just once, in Tell Hum, and never again – a kind of temple on wheels with ten pillars at the sides, five of them visible (fig. 51). Such a mobile tabernacle was mentioned only once in the traditions of Israel, in the form of the ark of the covenant, and no doubt that is the meaning of the reference.

On the other hand, no mosaic floors have been found in any of the synagogues of Galilee, usual as they were everywhere else in the east besides occurring, as mentioned above, in four synagogues in other parts of Palestine. The most important mosaics are in Naaran, where unfortunately all the figurative representations have as usual been destroyed, while another mosaic in Beth Alpha, which can be dated from an inscription to the time of Emperor Justinus I (518–527), is perfectly preserved but very degenerate in style and less important artistically. The two resemble each other in almost every detail of their designs, which cannot be coincidence. At this period there was a Jewish typology, a customary manner of representation, nowhere laid down in writing but still setting the standard. The mosaics of both synagogues contain two large pictorial areas, one behind the other. The front part shows the signs of the zodiac. The twelve sections containing the twelve signs radiate out from a central circle showing the very heathen figure of the sun god in his four-horse chariot. The signs bear Hebrew inscriptions and are definitely figurative, even including images of human beings, such as Virgo. The four seasons of the year, filling in the corners, are also shown as winged spirits. The second part shows a design found on Jewish gold glasses and the frescos of the Roman catacombs. It depicts the ark of the Torah between two seven-branched candlesticks, two lions, and the festive symbols already found separately on the sculptural decoration of synagogues. In the mosaic, however, they are flat, merely a part of the floor decoration like a carpet, and this stylistic difference of style casts considerable light on the history of the synagogues of Palestine.

The first scholarly study of them concluded that the Roman emperors Septimius Severus and Caracalla might have shown the Jews special favour by building them these synagogues. That theory would date the building to around 200 CE. More and more names of donors have now been found, to be added to the many already present in Hebrew inscriptions on the synagogues, including the name of one Judah the son of Ishmael, described as the donor responsible for building the synagogue of Chorazin, one of the most important, and Chorazin was laid waste by the beginning of the fourth century. The time of the two emperors mentioned above, which was indeed the most fortunate period experienced by the Jews of Palestine since the destruction of the temple, probably did encourage the construction of these first fine buildings. It is not surprising that some of the synagogues in the Diaspora were older. In Palestine itself, while the temple still stood and people could go there on pilgrimage as prescribed by the Law, no one would have wished to deprive it of its unique character by building extensive complexes for divine worship in outlying communities. There is much to support the idea that awed restraint of this kind prevailed. As soon as the temple was destroyed, however, building began on a series of magnificent synagogues, and we can trace the development of style in them. It leads from sculptural, rounded shapes to a flat effect, to a certain toning down and the imposition of schematic designs, and it is the same development that marks the way from Greek antiquity to the Byzantine Middle Ages throughout the eastern world. The most schematic work of all, the mosaic of Beth Alpha, is quite late, dating from the beginning of the sixth century. We do not need to prove that the architects and building workers were Jews in a country they inhabited any more than we need to prove that Italian churches were built by Italians and German cathedrals by Germans.

The artistic picture of Jewish Palestine in the centuries between the destruction of the temple and the Islamic conquest – for Jerusalem fell to the followers of Muhammad in 636 – does not reveal all its riches until we study not only urban planning and the building of synagogues but

FIG. 56 The so-called tomb of Absalom.

the tombs as well. In the late Jewish period, Palestine buried its dead in two kinds of tombs, the mausoleum and the catacomb, i.e. tombs built of masonry and tombs hollowed out of the rock. The two most interesting mausoleums are in the valley of Josaphat, and are in the tradition of the tombs of Absalom (fig. 56) and Zachariah. They are square towers with roofs in the shape of a cap-like cone and a small pyramid. The ornamental forms, again, are Greek temple pillars, and the whole structure is very familiar in the heathen world of late antiquity, where it is found in many variants. It is the type of the princely state tomb, here treated on a more modest scale, and it is descended from the famous mausoleum of Halicarnassus.

On the other hand, cave burial had been the traditional form of burial in Palestine ever since Abraham buried his wife in the cave of Machpelah. We know of the cave tomb from every period of Palestinian history, and the Talmud lays down precise directions for its design and use. It usually consisted of a roughly square entrance chamber in which the funeral rites were performed. On three sides of this area there were grave chambers with shafts called *kokim*. While tombs built of masonry bore carved ornamentation, these tombs cut in the rock were richly painted, and so we know that painting in Palestine at this period was in the style of the rest of the Hellenistic world. The aim, as in architecture, was for as much spatial expression as possible, but here it could not be real and had to be shown in pictures on the walls. The painting was impressionistic, using vigorous brush strokes to model figures sculpturally in a bright light and with plenty of space around them. This was the style of the painting found on the walls of the houses in Pompeii and Herculaneum. The finest works of late classical impressionism, however, are the portraits on the Egyptian mummies of the period, which easily rival or even outdo any modern portrait in vigour and activity. The source of this style lay in the Orient – we can say, with probability bordering on certainty, in Alexandria. The paintings of Palestine were provincial art, but in the same style. The oldest painted tombs are not in fact Jewish, but were created for a colony of Phoenicians who had settled in Mareshah, the city whose Hellenistic construction in the time of the Ptolemies has already been discussed. None the less, these tombs are characteristic of Palestinian art and are surely painted by indigenous artists. The inscriptions and names are Greek as well, not Phoenician. The entrance to the main tomb, the burial place of one Antagoras son of Zenodorus, who died in 119 BCE, is designed like a temple gateway (fig. 57). There are two large mourning amphorae, one on each side, with tables and torches beside them. The inevitable eagles are painted in the corners. Garlands and pictures of animals – a whole zoology, with the names of the animals added – feature in the frieze of the long corridor leading through the tomb. The absence of portraits is striking; they were not included as a matter of course until later. They have been found in a grave in Jerusalem, although it is not absolutely certain that it is Jewish. However, a famous and magnificent second-century grave in Palmyra (fig. 58) very probably is. This tomb was a large complex similar to the Mareshah type, but much more fully developed. There is a square ante-chamber with two wings opening off it, wings which are in fact two further burial chambers. The names of some of those buried here are definitely Jewish and even have the name of God included in them. Names such as Male son of Jadu son of Jadiabel, or Simon son of Abba, or Bathmalku, can only have belonged to Jews. But the cultural atmosphere in which they lived here in the Diaspora beyond the borders of their holy land was more heathen, its art filled with livelier ideas, or it would have been difficult for a picture undoubtedly drawn from heathen mythology to find its way into the semi-circle of the vault. Less incongruous are the paintings on the pillars between the tombs. On each, a winged genius stands on a plinth where animals are depicted, and holds the portrait of one of the dead within a wreath. A whole pillar is devoted to the life-size portrayal of a woman carrying her child. These portraits are remarkably true to life and are among the best we have from late antiquity. Their situation, painted on the pillars, does not detract at all from their almost speaking looks. Incidentally, the sarcophagi were decorated with relief work and some of them also bear portraits, but unfortunately these are in a very mutilated condition.

The Jewish Diaspora outside Palestine, the great chain of communities

FIG. 57 The tomb of Antagoras, from the Phoenician tombs in Mareshah.

FIG. 58 Interior of the catacomb of Palmyra.

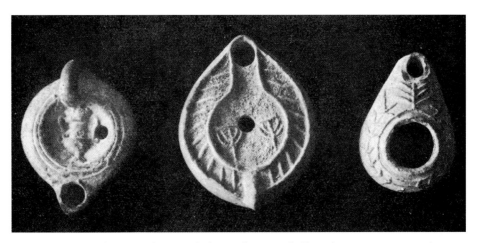

FIG. 59 Palestinian lamps of the Hellenistic (left) and Byzantine periods.
In the possession of Frau Emmy Roth, Berlin.

throughout the ancient world, was thus extremely significant for the art
of the motherland, where religious austerity meant that artistic interests
were nowhere near equal to those of the great lands of civilization. There
was a tradition of synagogue building in the Diaspora before the
destruction of the temple made synagogues in Palestine necessary at all.
The whole development of the community synagogue, which was
presumably the place of assembly too, a basilica within the agora, was
certainly not Palestinian. However, we cannot yet survey the manner in
which this development occurred or its history, the knottiest problem in
the whole history of Jewish art. For one thing, unfortunately we know
nothing about the Jewish community in the great Syrian cultural centre
of Antioch, or about the situation in Persia, although that country
harboured the great intellectual centres of Judaism for centuries. Nor
does the history of the Diaspora begin only with the destruction of the
last temple. There had been Jewish congregations in the lands of the
ancient world for hundreds of years, and although they acknowledged
the temple in Jerusalem as the one legitimate national sanctuary, they had
certainly created local centres of community life. We are best informed
about the neighbouring country of Egypt. From the records of a Jewish
military colony already existing in Leontopolis in Upper Egypt in the

FIG. 60 The temple of Onias,
model of reconstruction by Flinders-Petrie.

Persian period, we know that there was a Jewish temple there as early as the fifth century BCE. Ptolemy Lagi resettled a large colony in the harbour city of Alexandria in 301 BCE, and it became the most brilliant community of the Diaspora. In 154 BCE Onias, son of the high priest of the same name, who had taken refuge with Ptolemy Philopator in Alexandria, attempted (thereby incurring much disapproval) to build a subsidiary temple in Egypt, a temple 'like that in Jerusalem,' says Josephus, 'but smaller and less rich' (fig. 60). He describes it as being situated in the Heliopolis area, near a fortress, and shaped like a tower. It also imitated the temple of Jerusalem in its furnishings, except that the candelabrum was replaced by a golden lamp hanging from the ceiling. This again raises the question of the date of origin of the seven-branched candelabrum in Jerusalem. Despite all antagonism the temple of Onias, built in the Heliopolis area near Bubastis, continued in use until the year

71 CE, when it was robbed and closed down by Prefect Lupus of Egypt and finally looted by his successor Paulinus. Flinders-Petrie has found the site, still called Tell el Yehudiyeh today, and bearing traces of very ancient Jewish settlement. Excavations showed that the site corresponded exactly to the situation of the temple of Jerusalem, that its valleys resembled the Tyropoeon and Kidron valleys in Jerusalem, and that the layout itself was a perfect copy of the Antonia Mount and the temple with all its outer courts, although on a smaller scale. Anyone who sacrificed here, then, could believe he was looking at a replica of the holy places. Sacrificial remains have been found in large clay containers sunk in the ground, but no utensils and no remains of the building itself worth mentioning; the looting must have been extremely thorough. It has been possible only to trace the course of the bare walls, which were built of very well dressed stone blocks and give a precise ground plan. We know that the Jewish community rightly disapproved of this inauthentic sanctuary, which had a theatrical air about it, and it had no influence, unlike the great synagogue of Alexandria, praised in the Talmud as a wonder of the world. 'Rabbi Jehuda,' the Talmudic passage runs, 'says that he who had not seen the diplostoon of Alexandria has never seen a great wonder in Israel – like a great basilica, it had a stoa within a stoa, and sometimes held as many as went out of Egypt, and there were seventy-one cathedra of gold in it, corresponding to the seventy-one elders, and every one was made of twenty-five myriads of gold, and there was a bema of wood in the midst, and the officer of the synagogue stood in the corner and the sudarion was in his hand and [so another passage runs] when it was time to say Amen he waved the sudarion, and the people replied Amen.' This description illustrates the luxury of the building and its vast size, which made such a signal necessary. In particular, the exclusive use of technical expressions derived from Greek architecture is interesting, illustrating the degree of assimilation in the Hellenistic period, even if it was only external. The account agrees very well with the description of the synagogue of Tiberias and the finds made during excavations in Galilee. Obviously the synagogue of Alexandria was the prime model for Palestinian synagogues. Alexandria itself was certainly

FIG. 61 A Jewish jug of the Hellenistic period, Berlin.

the centre of the Jewish Orient and harboured its richest community. Two of its five quarters were inhabited by Jews, and there were forty-two other synagogues as well as this main synagogue, which was destroyed in the year 117 CE by the Roman legate Marcius Turbo.

Jewish mosaics, like heathen mosaics, must also have come from Alexandria. Jewish mosaic art in the east was not, of course, confined to Palestine; for instance, there is mention of a mosaic in Smyrna, although it has not been preserved. Basically, mosaic is simply painting with chips of coloured glass rather than brush strokes, and the very fact that the dabs of colour must be broader than in painting makes a particularly impressionistic effect. Mosaic was very popular in the entire area covered by these late Greek cultures. It is not surprising that Jews practised the art of mosaic, for glass working was very familiar to them, as it was to all Syria. Glass vessels of the finest workmanship have been found in the tombs of Mareshah. A Byzantine legend tells, with some malice, of a joker who made the sign of a cross over every vessel produced by a Jewish glass-blower, thereby causing it to break. A particularly fine glass

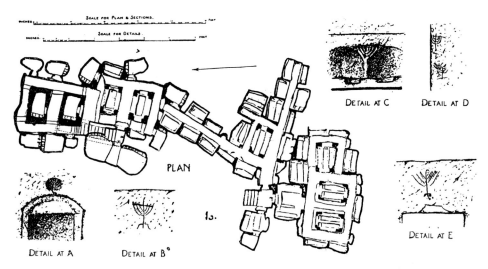

FIG. 62 Plan of the Jewish catacombs in Malta, and the depictions of the menorah in them.

jug of the period is now in Berlin (fig. 61). Extremely elegant, made of brownish-purple glass with a slender neck and a pinched lip, it bears Jewish symbols, notably the seven-branched candelabrum. It is therefore not surprising that we do in fact have a mosaic directly connected with the art of Jewish Alexandria.

It was found on Malta. The funerary sites of that island, the most important trading post on the way from Alexandria to Italy, show definite evidence of extensive early Jewish settlement. The settlers must have come from Alexandria. The Jewish community on Malta buried their dead in catacombs, vaults cut into the rock, after the fashion of the motherland (figs 62 and 63). In the Diaspora, however, the family vault was replaced by the community vault, so that the unity of the ground plan was lost. Clear planning, usually evident only in the first layout, was very soon followed by deeper penetration into the rock, with passages being cut to make space for more and more tombs along the walls. Becker, who investigated the island very thoroughly, has identified at least five groups of vaults in the catacomb of S. Agata as Jewish. The seven-branched candelabrum found scratched or carved into the wall near the entrance identifies them as certainly as any inscription could do. Otherwise,

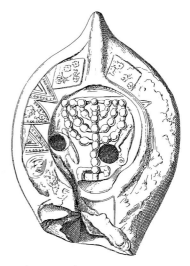

FIG. 63 (*left*) The Jewish catacombs in Malta.
FIG. 64 (*right*) Jewish lamp, Syracuse, the Museum.

however, they are unadorned and very sober, serious places. No
prescription was laid down for the form of tombs at the time; Malta,
unlike Palestine, does not know the typical *kokim* at all. The tombs in the
oldest, rather isolated complex are worked into the rock beneath beautiful
arches, and are tombs of the arcosolium type. In the four later complexes,
which are connected with each other and virtually form a single large
catacomb, the free-standing canopy over a sarcophagus is employed, as
well as deep vaults to which access is gained through a kind of window.
The effect, very architectonic, is almost like a row of chapels in the rock.
Of course these Jewish catacombs are not imitations of the Christian
catacombs, since they are older. They may date back to the Roman republic
and be entirely pre-Christian. This form of burial passed from Malta to
Sicily; Jewish catacombs of the same kind have been found in Syracuse
and near Noto. Particularly fine pottery lamps bearing the symbol of the

seven-branched candelabrum have been found here (fig. 64), and it was by this symbol that Jewish catacombs could be recognized thereafter.

However, the Jewish art of this time was obviously not just created to adorn synagogues and tombs. Again in Malta, a mosaic which clearly tells the story of Samson has been found in what must once have been a very luxurious villa (fig. 65). The artist chose to show the moment of greatest drama: a woman, beautiful in the Greek style, is bending back the head of an athletically built naked man. She has the scissors ready in her right hand, which she cunningly keeps concealed in the shadows. The narrative effect is excellent, as good, for instance, as that of the Laocoon group and as well modelled as any mosaic in Pompeii, where, incidentally, a painting with a rather parodic representation of the Judgement of Solomon has been found. The art of Pompeii and Malta both originally came from Alexandria.

This explains an extremely puzzling phenomenon which has recently led to many very wide-ranging studies. We have now given up attempting to seek the origin of Christian art exclusively in Rome, its later centre. (Joseph Strzygowski in Vienna was the pioneer here.) Like the origins of the new religion itself and its leading communities, those of its art lie in the east. Strzygowski has pointed out that the winged genii of the Palmyra catacomb are precursors of the angels bearing wreaths in the early Christian church mosaics of Rome. Even more striking is the fact that the most important series of pictures in early Christian art without exception show Old Testament subjects. They illustrate the historical books of the Old Testament practically verse by verse, with extraordinary vigour and genuine interest. For instance, the fourth-century wooden door of S. Ambrogio in Milan illustrates the story of David, the reliefs on the ivory throne of Archbishop Maximian (d. 556) in Ravenna depict the story of Joseph, and the great cycle of mosaics above the rows of pillars of S. Maria Maggiore in Rome, which are fifth-century at the latest, show the Old Testament up to the story of Joshua. Illuminated books follow the same trend even more exclusively, as in the Joshua scroll in the Vatican, the Genesis of Vienna, the Itala of Quedlinburg, the Utrecht Psalter and the so-called Ashburnham Pentateuch. These are all particularly early

Fig. 65 Samson and Delilah, mosaic in Malta.

works of medieval illumination, and their style is still wholly impressionistic; everything in them indicates the Oriental origin of their models at least. There must certainly have been social circles in the communities of the Jewish Diaspora, particularly in pleasure-loving Alexandria, which were unwilling to dispense with the luxuries and art of the Hellenes, and this is where we should seek the rise of Jewish mosaic work and book illumination. Naturally enough, these circles were also the first to turn to the new power of Christianity. The whole Hellenistic world was very like our own, in its flourishing art and its impressionistic style, and also in its uninhibited enjoyment of life, its scepticism, and its liberal attitude to religious tradition.

Here the second great problem of these centuries comes into view. Confrontation with Hellenism was followed almost immediately by confrontation with the new Christian community that had arisen from within Judaism itself. The outward differences, however, must not be seen as anything like so great as the inward differences, which only gradually emerged in all their clarity. Both religions were similarly set apart from the world of classical antiquity, showing the same hostility to its enjoyment of sensual pleasure. It was almost inevitable that early Christian art would share many features with Jewish art – for instance, catacomb burial and the basilical layout of the place of worship – which it then developed in its own way. Actual artistic expression was initially unimportant and irrelevant to Christian art too: this was the area in which Christianity had least reason to emphasize its special nature. The important point is that the centuries in which Christianity gradually gained ground and broadened its base are the same as those when the Jewish Diaspora was expanding most widely in the ancient world. Christian communities undoubtedly followed in the footsteps of their Jewish forerunners. The synagogues of Galilee and the most important synagogues in other communities of the Diaspora were built in the period between the crushing of Bar Kochba's uprising and the fourth century, a period also of crucial importance to Christianity.

The synagogue in itself, as mentioned above, probably antedates the Diaspora. The fine synagogue excavated on the island of Delos, the sacred

FIG. 66 The ruins of the synagogue of Delos:
on the right, the men's area, on the left, the women's area.

FIG. 67 The throne of the archisynagogos of the Delos community, front and side
views.

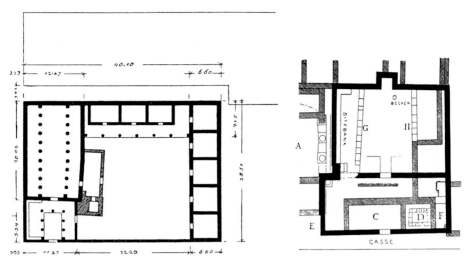

FIG. 68 (*left*) Ground plan of the synagogue of Miletus.
FIG. 69 (*right*) Ground plan of the synagogue of Priene.

isle of Apollo, certainly does. There was already a community here in the second century BCE, the time of the Ptolemies; Josephus records their privileges. The layout of their synagogue may easily date from this time, but even in its present form it belongs to the last century before our present reckoning. It was very well designed, with a ground plan of wonderful proportions. It lay not far from the river – synagogues in general were built near water for preference – and contained two main rooms: a large hall facing towards Jerusalem and a smaller room beside it, the two being linked by three openings. These were probably the men's and the women's synagogues. The Delian synagogue was not one large hall but a complex of many rooms. This difference between it and the Palestinian synagogues is in line with its general style, clearly more classical here in a genuinely Greek artistic area than in the area influenced by Alexandrian art, and more disinclined to Oriental splendour. Indulgence in two colonnades, the rule in Palestine, would have seemed undisciplined here. It is possible that the early origin of this synagogue is another reason for its distinction and restraint, and the ornamentation shows the same characteristics. The floor is paved with marble slabs, and there is a magnificent marble seat with legs ending in lion's paws by the west wall.

A white marble throne, one of the finest pieces preserved from antiquity, stands in the centre (fig. 67). It too has lion's paws for feet, tendrils wind along the armrests, and the same motif is gracefully repeated in the upright of the back and a footstool in front of it. Even the seats of the priests in the theatre of Dionysos at Athens were no more beautiful than this throne for the archisynagogos, the leader of the Delian synagogue. Figurative ornamentation, however, is avoided, obviously on purpose. There is another marble bench along the wall of the women's room opposite the prayer hall too. Washbasins and a cistern were naturally part of the equipment.

The synagogue in Miletus was built later (fig. 68). It too was constructed in a suitable place near the harbour, but on the ruins of a Hellenistic hall. It was probably not built until the fourth century. The ground plan is very like that of the Delian synagogue. Again, the women's synagogue adjoins the narrower wall of the main area. In Miletus we can tell that there were also pillared walks at the sides, and another ornamented marble bench in the women's synagogue ran along three walls. The whole building was designed around a courtyard. It was very imposing; the length of the front was forty metres. We also know where members of the Jewish community sat in the theatre of Delos; their seats are marked with inscriptions.

A third synagogue stood in Priene (fig. 69). (So far we know nothing for certain about the synagogue in Aegina, mentioned in the written records.) The synagogue of Priene was a basilical hall, very wide, with three naves divided by pillars. Here the niche was on the east wall, opposite the entrance. Its square shape, like its situation on the wall facing Jerusalem, suggests that it contained the ark of the Torah rather than the throne of the synagogue leader. The narrow ante-chamber could have been the women's synagogue. In Priene – and nowhere else in the cultural area of the Greek Mediterranean basin – remains of the sculptural furnishings of the synagogue have been found: the remnant of a pillar and two stone slabs. On all three, the seven-branched candelabrum is the chief symbol (fig. 70). On one of the slabs, found in the synagogue itself, it stands between two peacocks, while the other shows the two scrolls of the

FIG. 70 Relief from the synagogue of Priene.
Berlin, the Kaiser Friedrich Museum.

Torah lying beneath it, viewed narrow side on so that they simply look like spirals, and next to them are two of the festive symbols, on the left the *lulav* and *etrog*, on the right the shofar horn and the willow branch. The style is still very austere. There is no plasticity, none of the modelling that marked the ornamentation at Delos and even in the older synagogues of Palestine. The images lie on the surface as if cut from a flat layer, and seem so lifeless and devoid of feeling that one wonders whether the sculptor actually knew their significance. These slabs, like the whole building, which is not particularly fine, must be of the Byzantine period, perhaps the sixth century.

Jewry spread from the coasts of the Aegean, a area of Greek culture, to its artistic colonies, going north-east as far as the coastal towns of the Black Sea. Particularly in the Crimea, the ancient Greek land of settlement, many tomb inscriptions have been found with the sign of the seven-branched candelabrum. It – and not, for instance, the palm tree – was now the true symbol of Judaism. There is a lamp from North Africa showing a figure of Christ triumphant standing on a toppled seven-branched candelabrum. This is the first time we see the victory of the church over the synagogue represented, as it was to be shown so often in the Middle Ages.

The origin of this lamp leads to the area of the western Mediterranean basin, also an ancient land of culture, and one that had been much settled by Jews since the fall of Alexandria. One publication mentions no less than thirty-three Jewish inscriptions from the area of Carthage and Tunis alone. Many of them are tomb inscriptions from catacombs. The fact that this country has been far less scientifically studied than the east, and almost all the finds were made merely by chance, increases their value and allows us to hope for great things from what is yet unknown. The same is true of the one ancient synagogue of this area. It was discovered over fifty years ago in Hammam-Lif, formerly Naron near Carthage, and is probably the richest synagogue complex known to us from antiquity (fig. 71).

Again, it lay quite close to the sea, and was laid out very regularly, an approximately square building with sides about twenty metres long. Two entrances gave access to the interior. One was a small gate in the east wall from which a narrow passage led past smaller rooms to the prayer room, which was strikingly wide and had three naves. The passage led to the right-hand nave. The lateral naves were very unsymmetrical, the northern one being twice as wide as the southern one. We do not know whether they were divided from the central nave by anything but the divisions marked on the extremely rich mosaic of the floor. At any rate, there is no indication of places where columns might have stood. A semi-circular niche in the middle of the wall opposite the entrance marks the position of the synagogue leader's throne, where he would have been seeing the mosaic the right way on. As in all synagogues, the congregation at prayer faced the wall with the entrance in it, turning to Jerusalem even here in North Africa. The custom in Jewish synagogues, therefore, was exactly the opposite of that in churches. The niche in the wall was not an apse for the celebration of divine worship, but the place for the archisynagogos, and always faced in the direction of prayer. As in Delos and Miletus, there was a subsidiary room on the narrower right-hand side that can

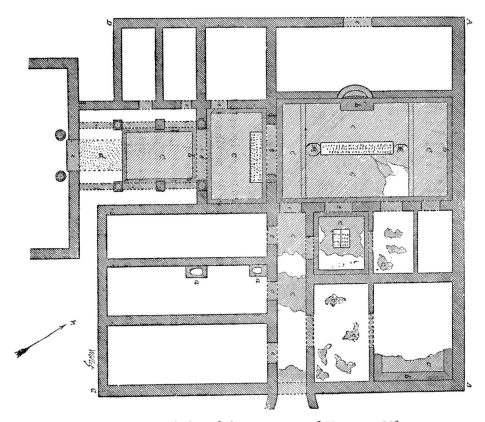

FIG. 71 Ground plan of the synagogue of Hammam-Lif.

only have been the place of prayer for the women. A wide opening allowed anyone inside to follow the service. This room was remarkably large, and women must have occupied a place of some importance in the community: the main mosaic was donated by a lady called Juliana.

The second, southern entrance was designed as the main façade, and was framed by two pillars carrying a pediment. A door between them led straight into a pillared courtyard which was directly connected with the women's synagogue. This courtyard must have been used as the summer synagogue, with the women's synagogue situated between both places of prayer. In view of the climate of the country it is not surprising that the summer courtyard was the main place of prayer. In all, the building contained no less than fifteen rooms, and was thus a genuine community centre. We cannot now establish their various purposes, except for a small

FIG. 72 Mosaic in the synagogue of Hammam-Lif.

FIG. 73 Inscription on the Hammam-Lif mosaic.

room behind the wall of the winter synagogue to which the community would have turned in prayer, and which according to an inscription on the mosaic floor contained the 'instruments of divine service', i.e. in particular the books.

The ground plan of the whole complex shows that it did not share the character of the Palestinian synagogues, which were large halls, but had developed from the community buildings of the Greek islands. There is thus a fundamental contrast between the Alexandrian and Delian types, and each had its own area of dispersal. Hammam-Lif, however, is a late building, as the mosaics on the floor clearly show.

These mosaics (figs 72, 73) are among the most important artistic monuments of Jewish antiquity, as significant in the west as the Palestinian mosaics are in the east. All the floors of the synagogue were covered with them, and among the images they show there is much familiar to us from African villas of the imperial period and not really appropriate to a synagogue, such as the busts of a spear-carrying man and woman. However, the floor of the place of prayer itself is entirely religious and extremely rich in images. In the central nave, an inscription divides it in two. This inscription runs right across the entire area, naming a woman called Juliana as the donor of the mosaic. The emblem of the seven-branched candelabrum frames it on both sides. Beside this symbol on the left-hand side the festive foliage and the shofar horn appear again, but obviously not very clearly. At this time, as we noticed earlier in discussing the relief in Priene, little effort was made to represent such symbols with verisimilitude – so little that on a seal where they appear in the same arrangement it has been claimed that they could represent the initial letters of the name of Christ.

The part of the mosaic behind this inscription has unfortunately been badly damaged. It is recognizably a seascape with fish, probably the main subject. The fish was regarded at that period as the symbol of the Messiah and has retained its place in Jewish customs to this day. The front part of the mosaic is better preserved. It shows peacocks between two palm trees and beside a fountain, with water rising from a large basin shaped like a krater or wine cup. The whole picture is intended as an allegory of the source of eternal life, and there also seem to be references to ideas of Paradise. This image again is linked to similar ideas in Christian communities, and is found frequently among them in ancient times. The images in the lateral areas, on the other hand, are purely ornamental. All kinds of animals, and baskets of good things to eat, are shown among acanthus tendrils meeting to form patterns of pointed ovals. Such images are common, even in handicrafts; the basic type is certainly Oriental, but by this period it had spread throughout the whole ancient world. It continued in use until well into the Middle Ages.

This same motif, however, proves that the synagogue as a building cannot be very early. There is no trace here of the freedom of movement found in Hellenistic pictures such as the Malta mosaic. Everything is clear-cut and hard, adapted to the surface. It is purely floor decoration.

FIGS 74 & 75 Mosaic floors in the synagogue of Elche (Spain).

The building must be fourth or fifth-century, about the same period as the Priene synagogue.

Further evidence of this is the fact that the inscriptions are all in Latin. We do not know for certain when that language took over in the Jewish communities of the west, finally supplanting Greek, but it cannot have been very early. On the opposite coast, in the Iberian peninsula, there is another mosaic floor, the remains of a synagogue, in the old harbour town of Elche (figs 74, 75). Again the division of the mosaic seems to be typical of the west, again the direction of prayer is towards Jerusalem, i.e. looking east, with the niche for the throne at the western end, and again the inscriptions of the mosaic are arranged so that the occupant of the throne would see them the right way up. But they are all in Greek, and they also name the offices of the synagogue, thus establishing the Jewish character of the building. The design of the mosaics is extremely beautiful and still classical. They are all ornamental, showing no non-Jewish subjects. The design is confined to intertwined and meandering patterns, coming together and parting again with great delicacy, and

FIG. 76 Jewish catacomb in the Vigna Randanini in Rome. Double chamber: arcosolium tombs on the right, niche tomb beyond, in the background.

ingeniously following the regular course of their frame in a way quite different from what would be found on a larger surface. Continuing our journey northward, we find Jewish symbols on seals in southern Gaul and in the Rhine area, and fourth-century fired red vessels (*terra sigillata*) from Andernach and Strasbourg which have friezes showing the repeated symbol of the seven-branched candelabrum.

There are good reasons why this journey through the Jewish artistic monuments of the Roman period should end in Rome itself. The city's Jewish communities, eleven of which are known to us by name from inscriptions, comprised some thirty thousand souls. However, Rome was not nearly as significant as Alexandria in the history of Jewish art. Rome ruled the world, but it was a political rather than an artistic centre. Its culture was that of the peoples of the Greek east that it had conquered, and it was less directly affected by shipping traffic than the harbours of the Mediterranean. Consequently, the art of an eastern people such as the Jews was much more likely to have its origins in the east and at the most undergo further development in Rome.

In proportion to the Jewish population itself, very little Roman Jewish art has been preserved . Throughout the centuries and to the present day, Rome has been a busy metropolis in which every new culture has been superimposed on what preceded it. So far, no remains of any Jewish building of antiquity have been found, and not a single Jewish mosaic, although the communities certainly did have synagogues. Nothing has been preserved except for several tombs. However, they are extremely interesting, and provide us with a good picture of the Jewish life of Rome in the first centuries of the present era.

To date, we know of six of these underground cemeteries. They lie together, according to legal prescription, outside the old city walls and, like other burial vaults, close to the major roads. As we would expect from the size of the Roman Jewish community, they were quite extensive. The oldest, outside the Porta Portuensis, the harbour gate, is very diverse and obviously still has features reminiscent of Palestine. There are cave-like rooms with small, deep cells for use as burial chambers, leading to individual burial chambers and galleries in the parts cut out of the rock later. The most important of the other catacombs are those of the Vigna Randanini near the Appian Way (fig. 76), the Via Labicana and the Via Nomentana. These complexes are of a more typical character, also adopted in Christian catacombs. Reached by steps leading down from a funerary building above the ground, they were probably all family burial vaults at first, later extended to become community vaults. Passages were gradually worked into the rock from the grottos, often even wider than those of the Christian catacombs, and new tombs and chambers were made along them. The whole complex thus became quite large, and in at least two cases, the catacombs of Monteverde and the Via Nomentana, they had two storeys. The manner of interment was very various. No less than eleven different kinds of tombs have been found in the Monteverde

FIG. 77 Ceiling fresco in the catacomb of the Vigna Randanini.

catacombs, the predominant types being the simple tomb sunk into the ground, the niche burial in the wall, and the arch burial or arcosolium. However, there are also bricked-up tombs, of the kind frequently found in Sicily, and coffins of marble and clay. The catacombs give a picture of a metropolitan community which has absorbed ideas and customs from far and wide. There were differences between rich and poor, of course, and the attitude of both individuals and communities to religious usage was as various as it is today.

The paintings on the walls of the vaults are so diverse that one is bound to conclude they represent different attitudes to religion. The ornamentation of the burial chambers of the catacombs in the Vigna Randanini is very like that of the oldest Christian catacombs, although without their Christian symbolism (figs 77, 78, 79). They divide wall from ceiling in the same way, with plain brush-strokes framing the surfaces. The framed areas contain peacocks and doves, even a picture of Pegasus,

FIG. 78 Pegasus, fresco in the catacomb of the Vigna Randanini.

and at the apex of the ceiling there are genii, one of them a female spirit carrying a cornucopia. These figures have symbolical significance. Derived from heathen mythology, they embody ideas that are not actually un-Jewish but were shared by all people of religious feeling in the Roman period. For instance, the peacock signifies resurrection and eternal life, while Pegasus soars up to the sun. The artists themselves must have trained in good Roman studios. The painting is excellent, the brushwork superlative in its ease and freedom, and the composition very well balanced. This is the international impressionistic style of around the second century, and a masterly hand was at work. On the other hand, the painting in the catacombs of the Via Nomentana is distinctly orthodox Jewish (fig. 80), deliberately emphasizing the unique position of the Jewish religion. All the familiar symbols are customary here, in their typical arrangement. The ark of the Torah is shown between two seven-branched candelabra on the back wall of an arcosolium. It is open, revealing the scrolls of the

FIG. 79 Peacock, fresco in the catacomb
of the Vigna Randanini.

Torah, which are unfortunately rather damaged – probably on purpose,
mutilated out of malice or during a persecution. They lie close together,
seen narrow side on to show the scroll shape. Between them, the other
symbols are shown separately, the palm branch and vessels of various
shapes being clearly visible.

FIG. 80 Jewish catacomb in Rome, in the Via Nomentana, arcosolium tomb.

FIG. 81 Jewish sarcophagus. Rome, the Lateran Museum.

This is exactly the same composition as in the mosaics of the Palestinian synagogues. Of course, the catacombs are older, and their history continues only until the fourth century at the latest. However, that need not make us conclude that this Jewish type originated in Rome and went on from there to Palestine. It is much more likely to have originated in the Greek cultural area, presumably Alexandria, and to have gone from there to both Rome and Palestine. The art of the catacombs as a whole provides the evidence.

Jewish sculpture on sarcophagi is also found, and again, it clearly expresses internal conflicts between different philosophies within the community.

The front of one sarcophagus shows the seven-branched candelabrum and its little lamps, much as it was shown on the Arch of Titus, but it is carried in a medallion by two winged genii, while others bearing baskets of flowers stand beside them (fig. 81). This is a type current throughout the Roman world from Cologne to Girgenti, although the medallions usually contain portraits of the dead. Even in Rome that obviously seemed too un-Jewish, although portrait sculptures do exist in Jewish catacombs. However, the Jewish patron who commissioned this work retained the genii, although they certainly express the idea of the happy soul in Paradise

FIG. 82 Jewish sarcophagus from Rome. Berlin, the Kaiser Friedrich Museum.

FIG. 83 Jewish sarcophagus. Rome, Villa Torlonia.

with the same type of religious feeling as went into the frescos of the catacombs of the Vigna Randanini.

Another sarcophagus, now in Berlin, is badly damaged, a particularly regrettable fact because it could have provided us with important information, since its images really do express the deepest Jewish feeling (fig. 82). The centre is occupied by the seven-branched candelabrum, again shown in great detail as it was on the Arch of Titus. There are two olive trees beside it. This was the principal image in Zechariah's prophetic

Fig. 84 Gravestone slab of Donatus, a cult official in the Bernaklesian synagogue. Rome, Jewish catacomb in Monteverde.

vision of the building of the second temple. Unfortunately, however, everything else is so badly broken that we cannot see whether the idea was carried through any further, although probably not. Some of the usual symbols can be made out: the shofar horn, *lulav, etrog* and willow branch, and perhaps the table for the sacred meal. This sarcophagus is made of particularly fine marble, and the style is so graceful and the shapes so well modelled that it must be of the second century at the latest. This early date is important in the history of Jewish symbolism.

A third sarcophagus has been found in the Villa Torlonia in the catacombs of the Via Nomentana (fig. 83). It is the finest of them all, and as orthodox as the paintings in these catacombs. The seven-branched candelabrum stands plain and austere in an empty space, with two small symbols, the festive foliage and *etrog*, at its sides. It shows how effective this symbolism could be when it appeared in all its abstract severity, without extraneous additions.

However, sarcophagi are rare, and obviously the Roman Jews tended to avoid sculptural ornamentation of their tombs. A grave was usually sealed only with a marble slab bearing the dead person's name, his rank in the community, and a few loving words. Some of the symbols, modestly carved, accompany these inscriptions (fig. 84). A hundred and eighty-four inscriptions have been found in the catacombs of Monteverde alone, and they incidentally show that the Jewish community in Rome was fully assimilated. Only the brief formula 'Peace to Israel' (Shalom al Iisrael) is found with any frequency in Hebrew; the main inscriptions are usually in Greek from the first to the third centuries, and in Latin in the third and fourth centuries. The names, however, show a tendency to preserve Hebrew forms, as is still the case today.

Among the smaller finds from the Jewish catacombs of Rome, lamps, glasses, ivory buttons and so forth, the most typical are the gold glasses. Gold-between-glasses would describe them more exactly, since two round, thin plates of glass lie on top of the other, protecting a design cut from thin gold leaf and laid between them. These pieces are usually regarded as the bottoms of goblets, but in a house in Pompeii, i.e. at a period before Titus's destruction of the temple, glass discs of this kind with erotic scenes depicted in gold were fitted to the wall of a house as decoration, so we may conclude that they also served as ornamentation on the walls of the catacombs, or marked the graves. It is certain that the technique came from the Greek east, very likely Alexandria again. The Moscow museum has a gold glass of this type showing a temple of Isis in the Hellenistic style.

This particular example links up with the most interesting of the Jewish gold glasses from Rome (fig. 85). It is the only one with a Greek inscription, and its style is so three-dimensional and colourful, so lively and interesting, that it must belong to the early period of the technique, and probably even antedates the Pompeian example. It shows not a symbolic circle but a landscape. A pillared court with a lattice-work barrier in front of it stands among huts and palm trees. It is viewed from above, in the manner usually adopted by eastern artists wishing to represent a large space pictorially. The middle of the courtyard is occupied by a building in the

FIG. 85 Jewish gold glass.
Rome, the Vatican.

Greek style, reached by a flight of steps. Four frontal columns support
the roof; the door to the interior is between the central pair. Pedimental
ornamentation is only indicated, but seems to suggest the seven-branched
candelabrum symbol. Two sturdy pillars at the sides, with bases and
capitals, shown very large, are either the pillars of Jachin and Boaz or the
two strange cedar climbing poles in the court of the second temple. For
there can be no doubt that this glass shows the temple of Jerusalem
among the people's huts and palm trees, and that it is 'the house of
peace' that 'shall receive the blessing' mentioned in the inscription. The
glass gives the impression of being a pilgrimage token brought by someone
from Jerusalem, even before the destruction of the second temple. The
symbols in the foreground are also shown realistically; the rigidity found
in Priene, Tunis, and even the synagogue reliefs in Palestine has not yet
set in. The seven-branched candelabrum in the middle is treated as one
of the utensils, and we can see the lamps and their flickering little red
flames, since several colours are used, not just gold leaf. Among the items
to right and left of it are the *lulav*, the *etrog*, and various vessels, in particular
two goblets with handles. One of them is probably the goblet of blessing.

On a late Byzantine design, however, echoing this type and showing its design as that of the temple of Jerusalem (in the Codex Amiatinus), a similar vessel stands in the temple courtyard and is described as a basin for washing, which judging by its shape it certainly is not. However, in a Jewish manuscript of the Middle Ages illuminated in Perpignan and now in Paris, the temple utensils include the vessel with manna and Aaron's miraculously sprouting staff, which according to the Biblical text was placed in the tabernacle. In the strict Judaism of the early Middle Ages, depictions of this kind were not original but traditional. Was there some idea that these relics were still present in the temple? And if so, is the original significance of the branch and amphora in Jewish symbolism perhaps to be understood in that sense? The interpretation of the amphora as a jug of oil for the seven-branched candelabrum, i.e. only one of the subsidiary, serving utensils, is very forced given its important position among the symbols; it must have meant something important. And does all this symbolism perhaps go back to representations of the temple of Jerusalem – which must surely have existed – and of pilgrimage to it, and is that why we find temple implements and festive symbols shown together?

However, the inscription provides food for thought. The word 'peace' in the catacombs always means peace in the world to come. 'Rest in peace', or merely, 'In peace', is a wish for the future found hundreds of times, at earlier periods in Hebrew and Greek, later in Latin. Probably, then, the picture is a mystic and pious concept: the eternal temple in the world to come, which has assumed the appearance of the national shrine. No doubt Jews had formed deep and mysterious ideas of the next world even then. A picture from another catacomb, steeped in the climate of thought of the time and probably belonging to a gnostic sect, shows the dead person being received into the next world in a pillared hall just like the one shown here. Such ideas of the world to come would not have been so very unusual.

The course taken by the development of Jewish art in the first centuries after the destruction of the temple, then, was neither simple nor superficial, but accompanied deeply emotional ideas. The transformation of religious

FIG. 86 Jewish gold glass from Rome.
Berlin, the Kaiser Friedrich Museum.

concepts brought about by the fall of the temple in Jerusalem was concluded only slowly, but in the later gold glasses of the third and fourth centuries (fig. 86), of which there are over half a dozen, the change of emphasis from service in the temple to veneration of the Torah is already complete. Only now do we see the full development of the significant symbolism of the Jewish religion in the opened ark of the Torah between two seven-branched candelabra or two lions; it occurs in small works of art like the glasses as well as in painting. Everything else is regarded as prehistory. The ark is always an architectonically constructed closet, the doors opening between its posts to show the scrolls of the scriptures. Their lack of adornment in all the depictions is surprising only to us. At this time all books were written on scrolls, so the shape in itself was nothing unusual. Indeed, it is likely that the scrolls lying side by side represent the different parts of the Bible, selected and read aloud according to the requirements of the day. At the time, much which was later performed to precise ritual, as a ceremony and a holy tradition, was still a living custom. Again, the backgrounds of the gold glasses are occupied by a varying selection of symbols, including the dove with the olive branch. In some of the glasses the lower part has become a separate pictorial area containing a table top with a fish lying on it, surrounded by a semicircle of cushions – the equipment for the repast on the eve of the Sabbath, the 'pure meal', to be eaten reclining and propped on cushions in the usual fashion of the time.

By now the glasses are completely stylized. Neither the Torah ark nor the table is three-dimensional; they simply lie on the glass, flat shapes in gold leaf, and are no longer pictures but symbols. Similarly, the good wishes in the inscriptions are almost always the same, and so is denticulated border. There are no more inscriptions in Hebrew and Greek. They are always in Latin, but often include Greek loan-words: the genuine polyglot jargon of a mixed metropolitan population. Their content is exclusively religious: 'Bibas cum eulogia', best translated as 'Drink and say the blessing'; very often 'Pie Zeses', also abbreviated to P.Z. and signifying 'Live piously', the word being taken in the sense of the Hebrew zedek. The longest inscription is on the fine gold glass in Berlin. It amounts to three lines, and is a dedication to one Vitalis, his wife and son. The glass was thus certainly made to commission.

Finds from the Christian catacombs correspond precisely to these small works of Jewish art – they show the same character and style, the same technique, sometimes the same formulae in the inscriptions, and differ only, of course, in the symbols. The Christian catacombs usually contain pictures of the first apostles, but otherwise the pieces could be from the same workshop. However, the important point is that gold glasses as early as the one showing the temple have not been found in any Christian catacomb. The Christian community of Rome seems to have adopted customs from the Jewish community.

At the end of this period, then, we face the critical question of how early Christian art is related to Hellenistic and Jewish art. Their meeting point is historically very interesting. Jewish art was now in its most flourishing period of development. Jewry was in the process of discovering new and final forms for its life in the Diaspora. Exiled from Jerusalem, it logically enough developed in the direction of abstract ideas, and the same course can be closely traced in its art. It led to the abandonment of all sensuous design, all the riches of invention and structure that had prevailed in the communities of the great Hellenistic artistic areas. In line with the severity of doctrinal teaching, only symbols were now tolerated, and those in a very austere form emphasizing their purely spiritual significance. This was the path to the Middle Ages.

At the time Christianity was forming its own community. We know that it was not immediately hostile to Judaism. Even around the year 100, it was expressly forbidden for Christians to pray in the synagogue. The outlook of Christianity itself was spiritually abstract and even more opposed to the sensuous than was Judaism. Accordingly it is quite natural for there to be similarities between the art of the Jewish and Christian worlds, for both to use the basilica as a house of God, to bury their dead in catacombs in the same kinds of vaults, for both to have the same burial gifts in common, lamps and gold glasses, and to share many symbols such as peacocks, the well of life and the palm tree. The firm definition of Christianity meant both the beginning of the Middle Ages and a new and very difficult time for Jewry.

CHAPTER FOUR

Goluss (Exile) and Ghetto

ISRAEL'S TRAGEDY was the fate of its dependence on other peoples. And it was indeed a matter of fate: the most objective historical investigation can allot no blame. The nation was no weaker, either physically or psychologically, than any other in the Near East, just smaller than the great world empire around it. Moreover, it had been led into the politically most dangerous place in Asia, the battleground that was Canaan. On the other hand, no trace is left today of the other peoples whom the Egyptians and Assyrians found in that country: the Philistines, the Hittites, the Amorites, even the Phoenicians. None of them had sufficient national strength, sufficient awareness of belonging together and being different, to maintain an identity as a distinct nation beyond the time of Alexander the Great. In Israel, however, national consciousness was extraordinarily strong. Even in exile Israel felt itself to be one, and religion was its strongest bond, the mark of its unique nature. Awareness of being a Jew remained a source of pride throughout the centuries – sometimes the only pride the nation possessed. For the world around Israel changed enormously, while Israel felt only the need to be the same, and its dependence on the world around it enmeshed it in innumerable fateful conflicts. As long as the international Roman empire continued in existence, the problem was relatively simple. Israel was dependent, in exile, but the circumstances of that exile were the same everywhere. The Jews were citizens of a world state within their single, world-wide community. However, the Roman empire fell, with only its eastern, Byzantine part remaining. During the period when the Priene synagogue was built and the Hammam-Lif mosaics created, conditions in the west had become very uncertain. With the westward emigration of Germanic tribes in the fourth century, agrarian states were formed everywhere. Here, people lived from the land; trade was very undeveloped and the way of life extremely primitive. Meanwhile Israel retained the tradition of the Hellenistic world, and was the only part of it to survive when the Romans were submerged in the Germanic states. It would be incorrect to suppose that the traditions of Israel were international, but they were those of a world empire with a wide outlook. It is very interesting to note that Burgundian law treated Jews as Romans. In the time of Charlemagne, the usefulness of their training in international politics was probably still appreciated. We know of diplomatic missions undertaken by German Jews at this period. Once penned in the narrow confines of the ghetto, all liberty curtailed, this tradition atrophied and became almost burdensome. Dispersal among other nations became enslavement by them in the Middle Ages, and gradually all free creativity and artistic drive perished.

For the first prerequisite of art is freedom: the right to create and to develop. Only a free man can create original works of art; those who are not free will reach at best the standard of their own time, and their products may be stylistically good, but no more. That is as true of nations as it is of people, and it is the reason why Israel never produced a style of its own again. Its art always adopted the styles of its environments, environments where other beliefs were held. It was Islamic, Gothic, Renaissance or Baroque.

The second prerequisite for a work of art is experience. The artist must not only feel if he is to create, he must also live in an environment providing him with the images in which he clothes his feelings. The field of vision of a Jew confined to the ghetto was extremely narrow, and became ever narrower over the centuries. Even worse was the fact that the most sensitive natures – always the most valuable artistically – were induced by universal scorn and the impossibility of achieving recognition to flee from the world, cutting themselves off from surroundings that showed them nothing but hatred. We speak today of the inferiority complex, but the typical ghetto neurosis was a tragedy of emotional wretchedness that can be heard echoing on even in Heinrich Heine. The most shattering evidence of it is to be found in the poetry of Süsskind of Trimberg, a Jewish poet of the Middle Ages, who also, at a time of relative freedom of movement, claimed to be a Minnesinger, but who finally withdrew that claim. From now on we can understand why post-exilic Jewish art was so exclusively concerned with small works, why the mind took refuge in books, while painting submerged itself in ornamentation and became the art of the miniature. Not only was there no sculpture or large-scale painting – it is as if architecture and works of craftsmanship also felt averse to large dimensions and grand effects. Of course there was building to be done, and the utensils required for divine worship kept many hands busy – Jewish architecture and Jewish crafts did exist – but just as the greatest achievement of the Jewish mind lies in religious scholarship and literature, book illumination occupies that place in art, although with great variation, depending on the amount of freedom permitted to Jews. On the whole, however, such an outlook was setting in even in antiquity, at the beginning of the post-exilic period, and it lasted until the liberation of Jews from the ghetto.

One can now see why the artistic culture of Judaism reached greater heights in the Muslim countries of the Middle Ages than in their Christian equivalents. The question of toleration or hostility is not exclusively religious, and there was no inner opposition between Muslims and Jews. They understood each other. Although Islam was at heart far more fanatical than Christianity, although it ruthlessly exterminated entire nations, it not only tolerated Jews but allowed them almost equal rights in its states. Hence the intellectual flowering of Israel in Islamic Egypt, North Africa and Spain, the roll-call of the brilliant names of philosophers, linguists, doctors, chemists and astronomers. It was Islam that actually took up and developed the culture of antiquity, while mediaeval Christianity rejected it, and the Jews were channels for that culture, were among those who conveyed it to Islam in its first centuries of existence and who later maintained it.

The Jewish art of the Islamic Middle Ages was indeed brilliant, as we can still see from two synagogues built in Toledo, in what was then the Islamic part of Spain. They have both been preserved because they were

FIG. 87   The synagogue in Toledo (now the church of S. Maria la Blanca), view of the naves.

FIG. 88 The synagogue in Toledo (now the church of S. Maria la Blanca),
diagonal view.

later converted for use as churches. Similarly, the great synagogue of Segovia, which is very like the great synagogue of Toledo, and the synagogues of Cordoba and Seville, are now disguised as Christian churches. At the most, we can only guess at the full range of Jewish architecture in Spain at the time.

The great synagogue of Toledo, now the church of S. Maria la Blanca, was probably built about 1200 (figs 87, 88). As an architectural achievement it is as significant as any mosque. There was always a difference between Graeco-Hellenistic and Judao-Hellenistic buildings, in that the constraints imposed on sculptural ornamentation did not allow the synagogues to display the full brilliance of their period. It was otherwise in Islam. The worlds of Islam and Judaism are related, for Islam too permits no sculptural adornment, and it was particularly orthodox on this point in its western domains. There is almost no Islamic sculpture or painting from countries west of Egypt, not even in books. All sensuous artistic feeling went into architecture and its ornamentation, which therefore became extremely animated, practically uncontrolled in style. One expects the purpose of a building to be expressed in its structures, but here the architecture transforms itself into an almost undisciplined tendency to take its structures and ornamentation to heights of ecstasy.

Consequently, the Toledo synagogue is notable not for disciplined order but for its suggestion of movement. The pillared arcades stand side by side, uninterrupted, following one another regularly in four equal rows forming five parallel naves. Movement permeates the smallest detail. The uprights are octagonal pillars, each a single unit. Their capitals are not designed as bearers for the arches but merely as interlinking members. On the capital, a band sets out from each corner of the pillar, intertwining with the next, following a complicated course and terminating in a volute. Each form seems to have neither beginning nor end, seems to be intertwined movement for no logical reason. The horseshoe-shaped arches characteristic of Spanish Islam rise above these pillars. They engage the eye in a very stimulating, indeed exciting way. The semi-circular arch of antiquity expressed equilibrium, resting on its pillars and vaulting up towards the load it carried. The horseshoe arch, however, resembles a hoop that has been forced inwards and might spring back at any moment. Above the arches, the regular progression of the frieze of stars and the row of windows in the women's gallery link these separate architectural members to the flowing movement of the frieze, so that for all its lively detail, the building as a whole is constructed with a clear, secure sense of order.

This style culminated in the second of the Spanish synagogues (figs 89, 90). It too is in Toledo. Samuel Abulafia, treasurer of Peter the Cruel, had it built for him by Rabbi Meir Abdeli between 1360 and 1366. A passage of his own led straight from his palace to this small private synagogue. It has a single nave, with a women's gallery and an exposed ceiling framework. The decoration is very rich, but the effect is flat by comparison with the older building. Intertwining tendrils separate two friezes bearing script (the most intellectual form of ornamentation possible, since its abstract form has intellectual significance in itself). There is a row of flat arcades above the friezes, with double pillars bearing indented arches. These forms are traced along the flat surface, but sculpturally superimposed in a number of layers, and the realistic ornamentation showing festoons of vines dominates the stylized tendrils. A new element has entered the style here, one that does not actually belong in Moorish art, the use of naturalistic foliage. It is a Gothic idea which arose from the ecclesiastical art of France, which was in its heyday at this point. Muslims maintained no connections with Christian France, but even in the eleventh century opposition to Islam had begun. In the thirteenth century the larger part of Spain was Christian, and cultural links with the north became so close that the broad current of Spanish art assumed increasingly Gothic forms (the Mudejar style). It was almost inevitable that Gothic would mingle with Islamic forms in the private synagogue of a Spanish king's Jewish minister, a man whose master had himself sought for a while to marry a French princess.

What appears a unique occurrence here, however, was actually a significant cultural phenomenon. It is clearer in book illumination than in architecture, for the ornamentation of books has none of the robust, massive quality that links a building's ornamentation to its material. The

FIG. 89 The synagogue of Samuel Abulafia, now the church of El Transito, Toledo.

FIG. 90 Ornamentation in the synagogue of Samuel Abulafia in Toledo.

book is pure intellect; letters are both form and sense. The very fact that they are such ornamental, expressive forms had made handwriting an art highly valued among all Oriental peoples, including Israel, so that scribes were regarded as artists. In the centuries of the Middle Ages, when every

FIG. 91 Decorative page from a Pentateuch copied in 930 CE
by Salomo Halevi Barbuya, a pupil of Said Bar Fergai Balkuk.
Leningrad, the Library.

book was still written by hand, people of cultivated tastes found the
book's beauty in the beauty of its script. So it became a work of art, and
reading was an aesthetic as well as an intellectual pleasure. Jewish scribes
made of their Hebrew script an expressive achievement that was perfectly
permissible in religious terms, and yet truly artistic. It was natural for

FIG. 92 The temple utensils, page from the Pentateuch of 930 CE
by Salomo Halevi Barbuya, Balkuk. Leningrad, the Library.

them to go on to illustration. The list of Jewish illuminated manuscripts
in the Middle Ages is truly impressive: it is as if the nation's entire artistic
drive went into them.

By a happy chance, parts of very early Jewish manuscripts have been
preserved in the *genisoth* of the Orient, those synagogue rooms where
books that could not be used were stored. The works of Jewish scribes in
Egypt and Syria around 900 CE are of positively classic beauty (figs 91–
95). The pages from the Pentateuch written in the year 930, probably in

FIG. 93 Decorative page of a tenth-century Egyptian manuscript with the name of its owner, Aaron son of Abraham. Beneath, part of another page of the same manuscript. Leningrad, the Library.

FIG. 94 Decorative page from a tenth-century Masorah from Cairo,
written for one Meborak the son of Zedaqa. Leningrad, the Library.

Cairo, by Salomo Halevi Barbuya, a pupil of Said Bar Fergai Balkuk,
hardly have any equal even in Islamic art. The style is remarkably grave
and the illustration always a part of the text, never just a playful flourish.
The script lies in a block on the parchment surface, framed by the simplest
of basic shapes: the arch of a portal, the square, the star, the quatrefoil,
all usually consisting of combinations of plain, straight, interlinked bands.
These frameworks contain script and ornamentation in the most delicate

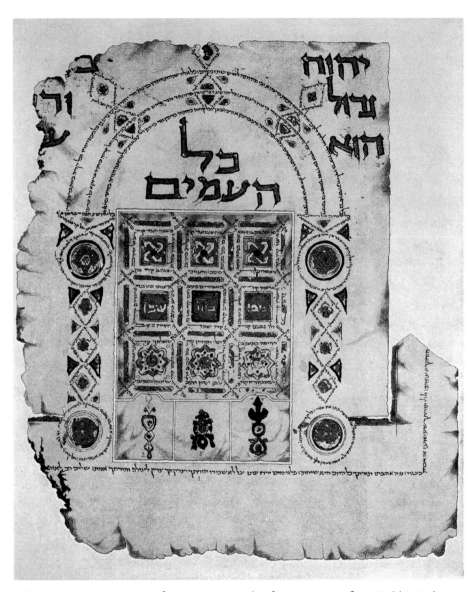

FIG. 95 Decorative page from a Pentateuch of 951, written for a Rabbi Nathan
and an elder called Isaac ben Joshua. Leningrad, the Library.

FIG. 96 Decorative pages from a Pentateuch of the thirteenth or fourteenth century, written in North Africa. Leningrad, the Library.

gradations. A dense structure of tendrils fills the larger spaces and the same pattern is arranged in rows in the strips. These are the austere tendril patterns of early Islamic ornamentation. A flower may venture over an edge, but every shape stands clearly in its place, and strict discipline is evident everywhere. Gold, bright yet solemn, is the main colour used on these magnificent pages, with now and then a strong, dark note of blue-black or red. The written word is taken very seriously. The name of the man who commissioned the work stands out with dignity, written in large letters, on a prominent page. Pictorial representations are intentionally avoided: only the vessels of the temple of Jerusalem seem to be depicted, not even the temple itself. Obviously the type of design found in the scene on the gold glass discussed in the last chapter derives from antiquity, for even the two mysterious pillars recur here.

These classic works help us to trace changes of style. The tectonics of the border structures dissolve. What were once pillars and arches become blank spaces, merely pointing the way to the written word. Grace supersedes strength. The drawing and the script become finer and finer. Clarity becomes delicacy, becomes calligraphy in the true sense. The lines

148

FIG. 97 Israel in Egypt. Above: forced labour.
Below: the story of Moses and Aaron.
From a Haggadah in the British Museum, London.

149

of the commentary entwine to form figures large and small, are made to resemble pictures of animals, play around the text. A sophisticated playfulness develops, affecting a style of microscopic writing that demands the utmost mastery of the technique.

With the coming of the thirteenth century, ornamentation in the area of Moorish influence becomes weightier (fig. 96). The tendrils and strips are coarser, more brightly coloured, and push out in front of the script. But the scribe still has enough wit to vary them. They are rustic, in line with the gradually increasing rusticity of culture in the Arab west, more related to fellaheen culture, and that very fact gives them a new strength. Remnants of such manuscripts from North Africa are extant, and there is a Hebrew Bible in a Spanish library which shows that Spain and North Africa were close in the art of their book illumination at the time.

At a later date the style of Spanish Jews living in the Islamic world diverges from the style of those living in the Christian world. The North African manuscripts continue the Moorish tradition. Tendrils fill the page, the writing set among them. But the same patterns are always shown, with the life and imagination clearly gone out of them.

It was very different in Spain itself. The Christian world in which the Jews of Spain were now living left its mark on the manuscripts, as it did on Samuel Abulafia's synagogue in Toledo. However, its influence was confined to ornamentation, and only the manuscripts tell us how deep it really went: they show not just the advent of new kinds of decoration, but pleasure in producing lavish series of pictures and illustrations to a text. Manuscripts acquired quite a different appearance without becoming any less cultured than those of the Islamic period, for in the Christian world of Spain Jews were still respected as scholars, just as they had been respected by the Muslims, so that they were in touch with the most artistically civilized circles in the country. They invented many of the astronomical seafaring instruments that made the American discoveries possible, putting Muslim science to the service of the rulers of Spain.

In Jewish manuscripts of the Spanish Gothic period, France was an even stronger influence than it was in architectural ornamentation. We have one Jewish manuscript of French provenance with sophisticated illustration of a kind that could come only from the best scriptoria working for the court itself (fig. 97). This particular manuscript, therefore, is probably not illustrated by a Jewish hand, but it does provide us with a criterion. One page shows cities being built in Egypt by Israelite forced labour, but there is no sign of any of the plagues; the painter would have no truck with realism. The aim of the period was to create beautiful, elegant books, and accordingly human figures of sophisticated appearance pose gracefully before a background of delicate ornamental lines, looking as if it were woven fabric. In the lower pictures on this page, Moses and Aaron appear before Pharaoh on his throne and work their miracles. Their fine, patriarchal faces give them the look of solemn priests. To us, who may seek for some expression of the story in the picture, it all looks a little artificial, but in its time it was a notable and particularly cultured achievement.

However, Jewish illuminated manuscripts valued such qualities so little that their robust style may be regarded as typical. This is true almost everywhere, in Germany as well as Spain. The Jew, who was not really very much interested in his environment in the Middle Ages but lived in his religion and his books, created very realistic, energetic pictures for those books and is thus, although independent, within the Christian artistic tradition of his time.

How do we explain this? First, by the peculiar position occupied by the Jews of the Middle Ages within their environment which, as is well enough known, could approach complete segregation. Enclosure in the ghetto, the obligation to wear special clothing, the prohibition on practising most professions that finally limited Jews almost exclusively to trade, barring them from working in any kind of craft, rose to the point of persecution, expulsion, torture and execution. Consequently, it was only to outward appearance that they lived in their environment and in their time. What they saw of contemporary art influenced them only in its general features. They had no access to such exclusively Christian experiences as the mysticism of the Gothic period. The Jewish artist, then, might be subject to the style of the time and country in which he lived, but merely in its most general aspect. He was a part of the stylistic circle whose structures surrounded him, but was independent in the finer points of content, which were entirely different from those of Christian art. Although some of the same Biblical books were used in both church and synagogue, there is no contentual correspondence in their illustrated manuscripts. The reasons lie very deep, and provide particularly cogent evidence of the unique nature of Jewish life in the Middle Ages.

Christian illuminated books were fundamentally monastic works. They were made for reasons of piety and for the purpose of divine worship: whole libraries of books were created with enormous industry, and illustrated with a devotion that cannot be too highly praised – but it was all outside the sphere of real life. However, real life is exactly where Jewish book illumination was most at home. Books for divine service were almost entirely devoid of art. The most important, the Torah, copied over and over again, had its rules precisely laid down: every feature was prescribed, down to the finishing touches of the individual letters. The imagination had no place here, and illustration of any kind was entirely excluded from the most important work of all. Other books intended for use in the synagogue also seem to have been illustrated only in exceptional cases: that is, if we do not regard the often extensive ornamentation of initials as a form of illustration. To take the case of an Old Testament devotional book: so far as I can discover there is only a single illustrated Jewish version of the Psalms, as against literally hundreds of illuminated copies by Christian miniaturists. There are very few illustrated Machzorim, and those that do exist are not very early. Similarly, the scroll of Esther, which was also read in the synagogue, is not found in lavishly illustrated versions until later. The Haggadah is a different matter: it is an illuminated book of Jewish art in the truest sense. A recent publication on the subject lists no less than a hundred and seven illustrated Haggadah manuscripts.

The reason for this is that the Haggadah was read aloud not in the synagogue, but at home. It is not a solemn text for recital at serious moments, more of a teaching aid for a child asking about the nature of customs he does not understand. There was always a great awareness of its content. Here we see the typically Jewish enjoyment of didacticism and teaching, which is very important to its art. The Haggadah met a

FIG. 98 Divine service in the synagogue, from a Spanish Haggadah
in the British Museum, London.

need for education by demonstration, something that seems natural to us
today, although the use of the rod commonly took its place in the Middle
Ages. The pictures in these Haggadahs provide explanations through the
clearest possible illustration. The painting is part of the actual content of
the book: it is in the nature of the pictures in a child's first primer rather
than illustration as such.

Besides these pictorial answers to questions, however, there are a great
many illustrations in the Haggadah manuscripts that have nothing to do

FIG. 99 Distributing the matzos, from a Spanish Haggadah
in the British Museum, London. *c.1200.*

with the Passover festival. Perhaps we can understand how the pleasure
taken by the illustrator, starting with the Exodus from Egypt, might lead
him on to the story of Moses and then back to Genesis. However, the
ritual itself is frequently depicted as the questioning child would have
seen it, and so is divine service in the synagogue (fig. 98), the exit from
divine service, the bringing out of the Torah scrolls and much more.
Here, there are almost no counterparts in the Christian books of the

154

Middle Ages. Even the celebration of mass is shown very rarely in relation to the number of illustrated books, and the Christian congregation is never shown at all. This is where the greatest difference lies. For the Jewish community is not just present at divine service, following it receptively, but participates through the synagogue officials, praying with them and making responses. The congregation takes an active part in Jewish worship, a part that extends into the home. And of the many acts of worship performed at home, the Passover feast is the most intimate. The Haggadah is not just a ritual but a family conversation, an exclusively domestic affair.

Consequently, a deep awareness of personal and collective existence became a creative force throughout the life of a Jew. It determined the way in which he participated in his religion, his dislike of dogmatism, the spirit of his literature, and above all it determined his art. In a period such as the Gothic, in Christian art a time of the utmost impersonal devotion, a very personal realism lives in the pictures of the Jewish manuscripts. It is not just chance that so many of them contain the names of scribes and owners, records of the place and date of writing, and many personal annotations. Individualism is a Jewish characteristic, and one that can be very creative.

This vigorous artistic sense broke through quite early. A Haggadah that must have been made in Spain around 1200 still preserves Islamic stylistic features, yet it is illustrated in a very modern way (fig. 99). A strict pattern of uninterrupted semi-palmette tendrils frames its sides, the horseshoe arch dominates its architectural representations, but the scenes shown are very lively. When the master of the house hands out the matzos, the emphasis is on the realistic clarity of the process. The painter shows it detail by detail. The head of the family has taken the unleavened bread from a basket in his left hand, a boy is taking a matzo, while another boy is already holding his in his hand and has turned to leave. The series of movements is almost cinematographic, and yet as clear as possible. The human figures are precisely outlined on the parchment. It is a straightforward record of facts.

In the high Gothic period, the middle of the thirteenth century, the

FIG. 100 Written page of a 13th-century Haggadah, now in Manchester.

differences from earlier manuscripts were only superficial. Jewish manuscripts of the time have the ornamented backgrounds, landscapes and architectural settings of the contemporary style, but the pictures retain their clarity (fig. 100). We can follow the progress of the new style clearly. The decorative pages lose their severity of outline and acquire greater richness. The borders are no longer such a rigid frame enclosing the page, but become decorative. Tendrils become more jagged, bearing leaves of thorny appearance frequently extending over the border and into the page. Strange fantasies begins to play around them. The grotesque hybrids of man, animal and plant known as *drôleries* haunt their curves and angles. Tendrils grow from headless bodies, men bearing crossbows have the hindquarters of a lion, birds and butterflies flutter among the tendrils, archers hunt fairy-tale birds among the swaying arabesques – all the ornamentation of the manuscripts has dissolved into movement. Sometimes the 'hare hunt', the *Hasenjagd*, is shown among the tendrils: in German the word contains the initial letters of everything needed for Kiddush, and later on the hare hunt becomes a standard part of the Jewish pictorial vocabulary. At this time, however, all these small grotesques are depicted only for their amusing deformities. The full-page pictures are a very different matter. They were felt to be important, and show purely Jewish subjects. The incidents illustrated here are the Exodus from Egypt, the story of Moses and its prehistory in Genesis, and of course the ceremonies of Seder and the festive service in the synagogue. All the subjects of the Haggadah illustrations were in the Franco-Hispanic mediaeval tradition.

The pictures containing the most genuine feeling are usually scenes of Jewish life, which is not surprising, since there were no models for them anywhere else in contemporary art. They had to be conceived and devised from nothing. These are true genre paintings of a kind found hardly anywhere else in the Middle Ages. If we compare them in a manuscript with the pictures of the Exodus from Egypt and the pursuit by Pharaoh's army, the difference between creation and convention stands out clearly. The procession of Egyptian warriors on foot and horseback is not very expressive. Their armour and weapons are precisely rendered, but

FIG. 101 Decorative page, from the Sarajevo Haggadah.

FIG. 102 (*left*) The four last days of creation, from the Sarajevo Haggadah.
FIG. 103 (*right*) The story of Adam and Eve, from the Sarajevo Haggadah.

everything else is in the conventional style of mediaeval chronicles. On the other hand, the Pesach preparations on other pages are wonderfully well observed, with characteristic touches such as the moments when the servant bends to slaughter the lamb, reaches out to paint the blood on the door, and industriously turns the meat on the spit over the fire.

The best known of these illuminated manuscripts, and certainly one of the most artistically valuable, is the Haggadah in Sarajevo Museum (figs 101–103). It is undoubtedly from Spain and dates from the latter part of the fourteenth century. The date can be determined from the style of ornamentation, with fantastic tendril designs of a kind found only in the high Gothic period. A wealth of individual details provide evidence of its Spanish origin. The pictures of the Seder evening ceremony convey very strong local colour. The lamps hanging from the ceiling and the bottle of wine on the table could be depicted in this particular way only in a Muslim country, and the picture of the family seated at the Seder

FIG. 104 (*left*) Above: the crossing of the Red Sea. Below: Miriam's dance.
FIG. 105 (*right*) Moses on Mount Sinai.

table, with a negro woman squatting on the floor beside them, shows the art of this time and place existing on the frontier between east and west.

The emotional world of the Jewish Middle Ages comes to vivid life in these pictures. There is no doubt that the artist himself was Jewish, as the artists illustrating Haggadas almost always were. The narrative of his pictures runs from right to left, like the script itself, and his mystical thinking is that of a Jew in the Middle Ages. The narrative proceeds from the creation of the world (fig. 102), shown as a kind of prologue, through Genesis to the story of Moses, and on to the Exodus. The series approaches its end with a solemn vision of the temple of the future, seen rather curiously as a citadel. Next comes the synagogue of the present with the scrolls of the Torah in the ark – open, as if in response to the congregation's desire for assurance – and only then does the Haggadah itself begin, with its pictures of ritual. The sacred is separated from the secular with a deep sense of visionary awe. Although the very first pictures, showing the days of creation, are very Gothic in style, in spirit they are entirely Jewish. Christian representations of the same subject depict God standing in front of the earth, shown as a small disc, blessing it while it puts out green leaves or brings forth living creatures. The Jewish scribe, however, shows nothing but the earth itself, making it look larger and the picture more significant. It fills the whole area, with the rays of the spirit of God descending on it and bringing forth life. The concept is not only very devout but truly cosmic in stature. In an evocative touch, the peace of the Sabbath on the seventh day is conveyed simply by the contemplative, quiet figure of a seated worshipper, whereas the art of the period as a whole does not shrink from showing God himself resting from his labours. The anthropomorphism of the Bible, speaking of God first in action and then resting, is raised in these pictures to the level of the eternal, and the episodic character of the words gains cosmic significance. The narrative now turns to the story of the first man and woman (fig. 103), care being taken to avoid showing either God or an angel. In fact the angel is even absent from the scene of Adam and Eve being expelled from Paradise, while Eve at her distaff and Adam ploughing his field are the start of a long series of very realistic scenes. The story of the patriarchs is told in detail, and the closer the pictures come to the fate of Israel in Egypt the more space is given to each narrative. The story of Joseph alone comprises ten pages showing nineteen episodes, depicted with the utmost realism. All the characters wear costumes of the artist's own time. The building of the tower of Babel is shown as if from the building site itself. Esau carries a crossbow, Pharaoh wears a crown like the crown of the king of France, and Joseph's prison is a dungeon in the tower of a citadel. This approach is not unusual in the Middle Ages, when art did not take the historical approach but regarded religion as something experienced in the present. However, Jewish book illumination differs in two fundamental ways from its Christian counterpart of the time. One difference arises from the religious philosophy of Judaism, residing in the consistent representation of the figures of God or an angel by flames or rays, or if it is absolutely essential to show angels (for instance with the angels on Jacob's ladder), by depicting them as headless

FIG. 106 For comparison: Noah's ark,
from the psalter of St Louis of France. *c.*1260.

winged beings. The other difference is an artistic one, consisting of the
sheer force of the realistic narrative at a period which was more inclined
to the graceful and elegant. The story of Joseph is a gripping one, the
pictures following one another like scenes in a drama, and Potiphar's
wife catches Joseph by his garment in a lifelike movement, just as Miriam's
dance conveys rhythm and the figure of Moses on Mount Sinai conveys
stature (figs 104, 105).

A comparison may serve to illustrate the artistic attitude of Jewish
book illumination of this kind in the context of contemporary art as a

whole. The psalter of St Louis of France is one of the formative works of the Gothic style (fig. 106). When the artist sets out to show the story of Noah and his ark, he first surrounds the page with a very graceful frame of tendril patterns, then constructs a work of Gothic architecture which is actually only another frame, and depicts the ark inside it. The ark is in cross-section, so that we can see exactly how many barrels and how many sacks of flour it carried to provision it, and what kinds of animals were on board – mammals in the lower storey and birds under the roof. Noah is looking out of a porthole, receiving the olive branch from the dove.

The Jewish manuscript dispenses with all superfluity and divides the page into two large areas (fig. 107). In the upper picture the ark is drifting on the waters, a closed chest with the rain pouring down around it, utterly inaccessible. In the lower picture, Noah has just come out on dry land. The story is very simply told, and to the French court would surely have looked rustic and unsophisticated. Yet I know of no picture in the entire history of art that expresses a sense of isolation in disaster as well as that closed ark with the wind and rain beating down on it. The very fact that these pages are so natural, so plain and uncontrived, gives them a stature usually lacking at the period. This robust strength speaks more eloquently to us today, with our experience of expressionism, than the sophisticated courtly painting of the same period.

After the expulsion of the Jews from Spain their artistic inheritance went to Italy. Not literally, since it had been too forcibly uprooted for many of its cultural assets to be transplanted. However, of the countries where the Jews driven from Spain found a home, only Italy developed a Jewish culture of similar importance, a further proof of the fact that art can exist only in a genuinely cultural atmosphere allowing the artist freedom to create. It was present here, even for Jews. The idea of a kind of civic freedom that could hold its own in the face of mediaeval concepts and claims first developed in Italy. It may be said that in practice, if not in law, Jewish citizens had equal rights in the great mercantile centres of the country, after the fifteenth century at least, and this was the time of the Renaissance and the heyday of Italian artistic and intellectual achievement.

FIG. 107 Above: Noah's ark in the flood.
Below: Noah leaving the ark.
From the Sarajevo Haggadah.

This complete freedom had a surprising effect on the art of Italian Jews: it became so Italian that it sometimes lacks any real Jewish colour at all. Its creations are simply those of Italian art on its own high level. This explains why it is particularly in Italy that doubts of the amount of Jewry's share in its own art have always been expressed. We have many products of Jewish art from Italy, but distinctions between Jews and Italians, at least in art, are virtually non-existent.

Even the mediaeval synagogues of Italy have taken on much of the character of their Italian environment. With the attractive pointed arches of its windows, the building that was probably once the synagogue of Trani, a major centre of Talmudic scholarship, resembles the palaces of the late Norman period, and the Gothic synagogues of Siena and Pesaro are turreted buildings of dressed stone like the large houses of the wealthy in those cities. It is noticeable that their exteriors do not suggest places of worship at all, standing modest and unassuming among the other buildings. To outward appearance, the Renaissance brought no changes, but it did bring inward change.

The Renaissance brought the revival of intellectual life, scholarship and the study of ancient literature. In this respect it consciously differed from the religious devotion that had been the hallmark of the Middle Ages. The new intellectual demand was for clear study and clear thinking. It says much for the sound judgement and genuine objectivity of this new philosophy, which opened up the way to modern thinking, that it did not stop short at the gates of the ghetto. The scholarship of the Jewish world, its medicine, astronomy and chemistry, were exact sciences like their Islamic counterparts, and they were now in demand. When the study of ancient languages reached Hebrew it needed the philological training of Jewish scholars. They even became leading figures, and their rôle in the intellectual world of Italy was as important as it had always been in the world of commerce.

The furnishings of Italian synagogues of the time comprise an impressive series of fine works of craftsmanship. The series begins with the Torah ark and the cantor's desk from the synagogue in Modena, now in the Musée Cluny in Paris (figs 108, 109). Their style is distinctly Gothic,

FIG. 108 Torah ark, from the synagogue of Modena.
Paris, the Musée Cluny.

and they are not designed for integrated effect: the wooden surfaces are constructed as small separate panels filled in with dense, deeply carved tracery. The entangled pattern is almost over-rich, more German than Italian. By 1505, the date of the Torah ark, this kind of ornamentation was impossible in Italy itself but not in the north, and German craftsmanship was found even in Venice.

Some twenty years later this style had been entirely superseded. Renaissance principles ruled in the synagogues of northern Italy as they

166

FIG. 109 The cantor's desk, from the synagogue of Modena.
Paris, the Musée Cluny.

167

FIG. 110 Renaissance Torah ark.
Paris, the Rothschild Collection in the Musée Cluny.

FIG. 111 Throne from the synagogue in Siena, wood and gilded stucco.
Berlin, the Schlossmuseum.

FIG. 112 The Scuola Spagnuola, Padua.

did in the rest of the country. A Torah ark now in Paris, from Reggio in northern Italy and thus close to Modena (fig 110), and a synagogue throne in Berlin, probably from Sienna (fig. 111), are typical of furnishings in the new style, imitating features from classical triumphal arches, temples and sarcophagi because only antiquity seemed to have sufficient human stature and importance. Classical columns and friezes, pilasters and pediments were adapted to the requirements of the time. The back of the throne –

FIG. 113 17th-century synagogue in Venice.

Fig. 114 Almemar, the Scuola Italiana, Padua.

FIG. 115 Torah ark and the seats for the rabbi and prayer leader,
the Scuola Italiana, Padua.

we do not know what its seat looked like – was flanked by two pilasters. Lavish acanthus ornamentation spills over into the main area and marks out the capitals. A sculptural frieze of griffins, flanked by candelabras of antique style, adds a powerful touch to the top of the throne. This top part, resting on consoles, projects to form a canopy. Like an echo, the same motif recurs lower down. All the ornamentation, picked out in gold on a blue ground, is very energetic. The Torah ark is even more impressive. It purpose requires a structural design unusual in Italy: it stands slender and tall on a firm base, framed by its two lateral pilasters and its frieze, while rich carving adorns the doors. I need hardly add that none of the carving is pictorial, consisting only of tendrils.

The series of works closes with the great Renaissance synagogues of northern Italy, particularly Venice and Padua, where Spanish, Italian and Ashkenazi Jews had separate synagogues, as they also did elsewhere in Italy. Perhaps the earliest is the Scuola Spagnuola in Padua (fig. 112). Its ceiling consists of exposed joists, as in the castles of the Tyrol, and there is still something very Gothic about this emphasis on the actual construction. The Renaissance synagogues, like contemporary churches, aim exclusively for effect and dignity. The great synagogue in Venice, a seventeenth-century building, has pilasters in the antique style in ceremonial array around the walls, and a heavy coffered ceiling, like that of the Doge's palace, is a powerful presence above the room (fig. 113). Similarly, the interior furnishing of the Scuola Italiana in Padua belongs to the mature style of the period. Its ceiling is very effectively divided into three parts, a large barrel vault flanked by flat coffered areas. This is the characteristic type of Baroque synagogue repeatedly found in similar forms in Amsterdam and central Germany. The almemar no longer stands in the middle of the nave, as it did in the Middle Ages, but against the wall like the altar of a church (fig. 114). It is an open chair with pillars supporting a kind of canopy over it. They are very slender, not shaped as if they were designed to bear weight. The furnishings are extremely impressive, and yet have an air of restraint about them, merely providing a setting for prayer and the reading of the Torah. The Torah ark has changed its shape a good deal (fig. 115). It is now intended to be the focal

FIG. 116 Chanukah candelabrum from the synagogue in Padua.

point and spiritual centre of the synagogue, and is solemnly enclosed by double Corinthian columns whose ceremonial massivity emphasizes its status. After 1600 the ornamentation of small tendril patterns that made the older furnishings look so lavishly decorated gives way to a great sense of religious dignity. The early Renaissance had already striven for

FIGS 117 & 118 Silver container for the Torah, shown closed and open,
Italian work. Paris, the Musée Cluny.

the noble grandeur of antiquity, and now it had attained that end.

All the magnificence of interior synagogue decoration in these rich
Italian communities must be mentioned if we are to see the picture
complete. We must imagine the floors covered with the most beautiful

Persian carpets, which were just being brought to the west at this time by the Jewish Levantine trade. We know that the great Persian carpet with its animal design which is the jewel of the Islamic Collection in Berlin once covered the floor of the Genoa synagogue. No one objected to the animals and arabesques in the pattern, but the human figures who happened to be shown at the corners were cut away. The other most important items of synagogue furnishing were the candelabra and candlesticks. They were needed for services held in the evening and at night and were of particularly luxurious manufacture. A fine bronze Chanukah candelabrum from the synagogue in Padua has been preserved (fig. 116). It rises on a slender stem and divides into branching arms bearing their cups like flowers. In addition, a wide range of Torah ornaments and embroideries from Italian synagogues exists and is still comparatively unknown (figs 117, 118, 119). There were also many Jewish potters whose Seder dishes are examples of fine Italian majolica ware of the sixteenth to the eighteenth century. In particular, several generations of the Azulai family made them. This family came from Spain, and their name suggests that before the expulsion they were already making beautiful faience tiles of the kind that adorn the walls of Moorish rooms. Since faience manufacture in Italy was in fact inspired by this technique, it may be that the Jews expelled from Spain played a part in bringing the craft to Italy. It called for a thorough knowledge of chemistry and was jealously guarded as a precious asset.

The significance of the art of the Italian synagogues leads one to expect the greatest perfection in manuscripts. Italy itself set a very high value on beautifully decorated books. It was fashionable to own manuscripts and employ scribes to make them, and it could be assumed that the Jews of Italy would not lag behind in this, their special province. Indeed, their manuscripts are classic works of Italian book illumination by Jewish hands, all the more important because this was the only kind of painting – and painting was the major art of Italy in the age of Raphael and Michelangelo – that was permitted in the Jewish religion. Consequently the range of works illustrated is particularly large in Italy. Books of ritual, the philosophical writings of Maimonides, the Machzor,

FIG. 119   Italian Chanukah candelabrum
(on the top is a copy of Benvenuto Cellini's Perseus). Paris, the Musée Cluny.

the Sziddur, of course the Haggadah, and many other works were illustrated with miniatures. The range of possibilities for an artist had been extended so far in Italy that we can say they stopped short only at the scrolls of the Torah.

The style had changed completely from that of the Middle Ages, in line with the new thinking of this period. The mediaeval practice of treating paintings in books as ornamentation, scattering them through the text and linking them with it, had been completely abandoned. A picture in a book was kept as firmly in its place as the picture on the altar. This made sense in that it was a concept separate from the text. The logic of the period demanded the illusion of reality in a picture; it existed on its own, apart from the words.

This inevitably meant the disappearance of the *drôleries*. The tendrils inside the frames were now crowded together in a solid block. The initials were not just outsize but vigorous and magnificent. Similarly, man and his environment became an important subject of study. The great discoveries of the Florentine and the Venetian painters had taught artists to depict space and the landscape in perspective, setting human figures in that perspective and showing movement correctly. Line drawing and backgrounds of gold leaf were now finally abandoned, and man stepped into the centre of art.

In a manuscript in the Rothschild Collection in Paris which contains readings from the Bible, the Sziddur and the Haggadah, the pictures clearly show the strength of the endeavour to create not just illustrations but small-scale paintings. They depict Biblical incidents found nowhere else in a Haggadah. The artist's own imagination has created them from the text without feeling bound to tradition. A picture of the three angels visiting Abraham is particularly revealing (fig. 120). The angels appear as three winged beings behind the table, with Abraham in front of it, serving them. The composition is spacious, and very fine in the self-contained group of the three angels, held together by the central figure to which the other two are turning. No Jewish manuscript had ever ventured to depict angels as winged spirits before, but such a representation is obviously felt to be perfectly natural here, and thereafter angels were

FIG. 120 From an Italian manuscript.
The angels with Abraham.
Esther summons the people.
The destruction of Sodom.
Haman hanging on the gallows.
Paris, the Rothschild Collection.

FIG. 121 Preparations for Passover, from an Italian manuscript.
Paris, the Rothschild Collection.

quite at home in Jewish art. In the destruction of Sodom, shown below this picture, another angel is pouring out fire over the city, and here again form and content, the daring of the depiction and the assurance of the spatial composition, are entirely in the spirit of the new times. The story of Esther follows on another page. When the queen is gathering the community together to fast, her dignity as she faces the crowd is truly regal. The hall of her palace stretches a long way back, its perspective perfectly mastered. The picture thus gives an impression of breadth and reality, and the solitary figure of Haman condemned and hanging from a tree is astonishing in its tragic stature. This last picture, which literally follows the Hebrew text, allows the painter to display his knowledge of it. He must have been a Jew himself, and indeed there are many mentions of Jewish artists in Italian writings, so it is not surprising that the realistic pictures of the Passover festival in the Rothschild manuscript are as good as those taken from Biblical history (fig. 121). They are in fact rather unusual for Italy, where everyday realism was not a part of art, but they too bear the stamp of the great new artistic style. The baking of the matzos is divided into separate scenes to show the procedure in detail, and with great confidence. These are no mere illustrative flourishes but true accounts. Everything about this manuscript is masterly. Its place of origin has been suggested as Ferrara, which is quite possible – not only did many Jews live there, but they had much contact with the world around them. We even know of a very highly esteemed painter, Lorenzo Costa, who signed a picture in Hebrew.

The modern craft of Jewish book printing also developed in northern Italy. The oldest printed books from Mantua and Venice date from the fifteenth century, when the finest illustrated manuscripts were still being created. Any idea that the two methods were inimical to each other emerged only gradually. At first only the technique changed, the fine brushstrokes of illuminated books being replaced by the coarser lines of woodcuts, black and forceful on the paper (fig. 122). A sign of the changing needs of the times is a petition of 1521 by the Jewish painter Mose di Castellazzo for his sons to be granted privileges as woodcut artists in Venice. However, genuine Jewish works of art were created in this new

FIG. 122 Rabbi Akiba, woodcut after Michelangelo's Jeremiah in the Mantua Haggadah, 1560.

technique only in the initial stages. While book printing elsewhere brought with it a plethora of illustrators providing woodcuts, engravings and ultimately etchings, in the Jewish world, with very few exceptions, the technique of printing alone was adopted, and on a very wide scale. So much was read and studied in Jewry that printing could hardly keep up with all the material wanted, and as early as the seventeenth century books were almost entirely dispensing with illustration. Possibly there was a fear that illustrated books could not be sold to the devout. However that may be, in Jewry the printed book not only killed miniature painting – it did that everywhere – it almost killed book illustration altogether.

The character of Jewish art further north, in Germany, is deeply and fundamentally different from the character of Jewish art in the south. It is possible that the racial difference between Sephardim and Ashkenazim had something to do with it, and so of course did the difference between southern and northern art in general – but the deepest reason lies in the difference of their historical destinies. Spain had seen the great disaster of the expulsion of Jews from the country, and there had been much persecution and hostility in Italy, but never the terrible series of mental tortures that Germany inflicted on the Jews from the Middle Ages onwards. Their sufferings comprised not only the persecution of the crusades, expulsions and massacres, but even worse the mental torment of segregation, contempt, scorn and desecration, driving Jews to the loss of all self-assurance because they had absolutely no means of defending themselves. Jewry experienced its worst sufferings in Germany, where it was pilloried for centuries, although innocent. No wonder that its art in that environment had nothing like the freedom it showed in Spain and Italy.

The first expression of this attitude was in its places of worship. Germany had no magnificent synagogues such as those of Toledo or Padua, only modest prayer houses. Fortunately, enough of them have been either preserved or recorded in old pictures for us to be able to see what the architectural type was like and trace its development through successive mediaeval styles.

The oldest German synagogues are found on the Rhine, in those ancient communities whose history was especially significant and tragic. Only a synagogue wall still stands in Speyer, while at least the course of the walls and the niche for the Torah ark have been preserved in Rufach in Alsace, and the whole of the old building stands in Worms (fig. 123). As an example of mediaeval synagogue building, it is the most important monument of Jewish art in Germany. Its dates have been established – the room for the men, i.e. the main building, was built in 1175, the women's bath in 1186 and the women's synagogue in 1213. The entire complex therefore belongs to the period of the Romanesque style, which was particularly austere. Everything about it was practical: every structural element displayed the logic of its function in its design. There can be no greater contrast than between this style and the freedom of Islamic architecture.

The synagogue in Worms is a rectangular room divided by two strong Romanesque columns standing at the central axis and bearing the vault. In Christian ecclesiastical architecture it would be described as having a double nave. Here, however, the almemar stood in the middle, to a certain extent enclosed by the two pillars, and as the benches faced away from the walls and towards the almemar, the plan would be described as a central layout with two central supports. The difference between this type and that of the Christian church is very clear. In the latter, the altar stands at the end of the nave with the congregation before it, while the reader's desk in the synagogue always stands in the middle of the congregation. The architectural type is really a hall. Again, it is conspicuously similar to the basic synagogue plan of antiquity which

FIG. 123 Interior of the Romanesque synagogue in Worms.

FIG. 124 Romanesque portal of the synagogue in Worms.

had developed out of the place of assembly, and it shows how little
Israel's requirements of its synagogues had altered. The women's
synagogue was built against the north wall, also as a 'double nave', with
only one central column and window-like apertures through which the
women could follow the men's service. Again, this subsidiary building is
very reminiscent of the synagogues of antiquity in the western world,
where it was more like a lateral wing than a nave, for instance in Delos.

The architecture is in the same style as the cathedral of Worms and its
Christian churches. A fine portal led to the men's synagogue from the
north side (fig. 124), not from the narrower façade, as in churches. It
receded gradually into the wall, arch by arch, as if calling on the people
to enter and leading them in. There is little ornamentation here except on
the capitals and some very sparse remnants on the arches. On the other
hand, the interior columns are very much in the full Romanesque style,
divided into base, shaft and capital. Their function of supporting, bearing
and carrying a load is obvious to the observer. The capitals themselves

are divided into the main body of the capital and a linking member above (the impost or springer). Rich ornamentation, derived from the Corinthian style of antiquity, adorns them without impairing their power. They bear Hebrew inscriptions. The stone-carver at least must have been Jewish.

The women's bath (*mikveh*) offered less opportunity for artistic design. Providing for its ritual purpose was of more technical than artistic interest. A succession of spaces had to be arranged so as to lead down from the ground floor to the water itself. The plan was carried out functionally, without adornment or concealment. A flight of steps leads to a long room with a barrel vault in the ceiling, containing niches where the women could sit along the walls as they waited to bathe. The way then continues uninterrupted along a passage to the square changing room and on to the tower-like bath, whose vertical design, coming as the conclusion to the series of rooms, produces a fine effect. The synagogues of Speyer and Offenburg had similar designs for this area of the synagogue, and in smaller communities, such as Friedberg in Hesse, and in the rather later Andernach *mikveh*, the design could be curtailed to comprise only the tower.

The layout of the synagogue of Worms seems to have been as typical of Jewish places of worship as the basilical plan was of Romanesque churches. The spirit of the Middle Ages valued traditional form above personal creativity. The centrally planned synagogue survives until well into the Gothic period and remains the standard for all synagogues known to us.

The classic Gothic synagogue of Germany is the Altneuschule in Prague (fig. 125). Its interior too is a hall with two supporting structures and a vault (fig. 126). However, by now the forms are those of the new Gothic style at its height. The supports are no longer columns but pillars with angular edges, the ceiling is vaulted with ribs in the shape of pointed arches. However, four or five ribs do not come together in each keystone as they do in Christian churches: two windows in the exterior wall are situated between the pillars at the centre of each arch, with a special rib fitted between them on a console. We cannot tell whether the purpose was simply to accommodate the windows, or whether a desire to avoid the shape of a cross in the vaulting played some part, but probably the

FIG. 125 The Altneuschule and the Jewish Rathaus, Prague.

FIG. 126 Interior of the Altneuschule, Prague.
From an engraving in the art collection of
the Jewish Community of Berlin.

FIG. 127 The mediaeval portal of the Altneuschule, Prague.

FIG. 128 The Torah ark of the Altneuschule.

latter, since the identical feature is found in the ceiling of the Miltenburg
synagogue of the same period, and like the ground plan it seems to be
characteristic of German Gothic synagogues.

FIG. 129 (*left*) Interior of the Regensburg synagogue, from an etching
by Albrecht Altdorfer.

FIG. 130 (*right*) View of the vestibule of the Regensburg synagogue,
from an etching by Albrecht Altdorfer.

In ornamentation, the stylized tendrils of the synagogue in Worms
have been replaced by the life-like foliage which in Prague, as everywhere else, is a feature of the change from the Romanesque to the Gothic
style. A comparison of the portals of Worms (fig. 124) and Prague (fig.
127) illustrates the difference particularly clearly: the Prague portal is
very tall, rising between slender pillars to a high pointed arch, while the
Worms portal is solid and compact. The tympanon in Prague is decorated
with tendrils of ivy rising from a small hillock, branching off in all directions and filling the entire area with the movement of its jagged leaves.
Foliage of this jagged design appears on all structural elements that are
not for directly tectonic purposes, which means everywhere except on
the capitals of the portal, the consoles, keystones and the pointed pediment above the ark, where the motif is of vine leaves (fig. 128). A liking
for the ingeniously pointed form is as evident here as in the Gothic manu-

scripts, and here too the tendrils are distributed with great delicacy over the various surfaces and areas. The massed tendrils in Prague show as refined a taste as those on the very similar portals of Halberstadt and Magdeburg, and Meissen has a related example. This style of ornamentation must have reached Bohemia by this route, going up the Elbe. It was accompanied everywhere else by figurative sculpture, but again, that was strictly avoided in the Prague synagogue, whose date may coincide with that of the Saxon buildings. The Altneuschule synagogue in Prague was very probably built after the two great fires of 1316, but repairs were necessary by 1389, and the building was extensively renovated later. The octagonal form of the pillars is as much of a late Gothic conversion as the brick pediment on the outside.

There was a whole group of Gothic synagogues of the same basic type related to these particularly important buildings. Many were demolished only recently, as we moved into the modern era and the ancient monuments of all cities fell victim to urban growth. The synagogues of the congregations of Bamberg and Miltenberg have been preserved, although with many alterations, and the synagogue on the Kazmierz in Cracow is also relatively well preserved. Like the Prague synagogue, it is a hall with two central pillars and ribbed vaulting, showing that this was indeed the standard ground plan, a design reaching far to the east. We also have some idea of the appearance of the Regensburg synagogue; it was recorded for posterity by Albrecht Altdorfer in two of his finest etchings in 1519, the year of its destruction (figs 129, 130). Of course the etchings are not absolutely faithful to the original. Intentionally or unintentionally, the style of the artist's own time is bound to have an influence on such representations, although Altdorfer remained very objective and his etchings display none of the hatred that accompanied the destruction of the synagogue. As a result, some of the designs appear taller and more ornate than they actually were, for if this synagogue was completed as early as 1227 it is almost a century older than the Prague synagogue, as indeed it must be. The interior again was a double-naved hall, but this time with three instead of two columns, and very impressive. The columns bore Romanesque wall arches resting on pillars in several sections

Fig. 131 Silver spice boxes of Gothic design. Paris, the Musée Cluny.

at the sides of the synagogue. The vaulting itself was still austere in style, without any Gothic ribs. The vestibule may be a later addition, but the portal is probably shown as taller than it really was, and the interior seems too tall as well. All things considered, the building must have been closer in both date and style to the synagogue of Worms than the Prague synagogue.

The contrast between the Jewish art of Germany and that of the Mediterranean countries was too great to have been confined to architecture. The differences between their synagogues are evident in the

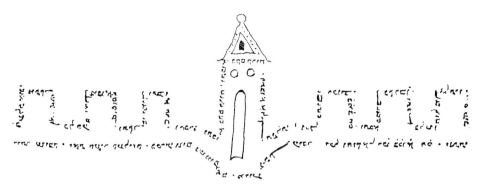

FIG. 132 12th-century figural Masorah. Germany or France.

synagogue utensils too. They were very much more modest in Germany, quite small items of craftsmanship, like the spice boxes in the shape of Gothic towers (fig. 131). The real meaning of the difference, however, becomes clear in the most characteristic of Jewish arts, the making of books. For the unassuming appearance of German synagogues does not denote less feeling for religion or spirituality; it is simply the consequence of outward constraint, turning forces inwards. Spanish Jews before the expulsion and Italian Jews of the Renaissance could turn part of their vital energy outwards, transforming it into impressive forms. That was out of the question for German Jews. Their entire fate forced them in on themselves, and all their interests were directed to the intellectual sphere. Such a great shift of intellectual weight is seldom a healthy process. When outward, sensual existence is excluded as unimportant, all imaginative power and fantasy is forced into the world of the mind. Mysticism takes the place of opinion, dialectic takes the place of criticism, analysis takes the place of creative multiplication. It is no coincidence that the Jewish art of book illustration in the north is so much more complicated than in the south, whose clear and simple manner one would seek in vain in Germany. And yet Germany is much richer in this field, with a capacity for spiritual experience that the south, in its turn, does not possess.

By now we can see why book illustration began so late in Germany. People were too earnest, their fate too harsh, for them to play with the sacred words. During the heyday of Spanish Judaism great communities also existed in Germany, but how could there be any joy in life, any pleasure in playing games with religious ideas, in a country that had brought the martyrdoms of the first crusades? Consequently the Jewish art of miniature painting in Germany began late and hesitantly. Purely ornamental decoration predominates at first (fig. 132). It is not surprising that it was a German scriptural scholar, Rabbi Jehuda ben Samuel the Pious of Speyer, who warned in the twelfth century that anyone commissioning a copy of the Masorah from a scribe should make sure it was not written in the shape of animals – an artistic game very popular throughout the Middle Ages and one which gave no offence at all in the east. About a century later, Rabbi Meir of Rothenburg feared that drawings of animals and birds in prayer books would distract the mind from devotion, and of course he was right. It sounds like a deliberate attack on *drôleries* in Jewish books, even though all other countries had accepted them and by now they had reached Germany. The literature and the facts are in agreement here. These stern warnings come at just the same period as the first appearance in Germany of paintings in Jewish books.

The thirteenth century is an important time for German Jews, a moment when they paused to take breath. After the persecutions of the first crusades, their political position in the Holy Roman Empire had been made relatively secure by the establishment of the system known as *Kammerknechtschaft*, which meant that in return for payment of a tax they were directly dependent on the emperor, and had his protection. At least that made them feel more secure. This calmer period coincides with a great artistic movement to the Gothic style, which meant artistic liberation from the austerity of the early Middle Ages. These two stimulating factors created German Jewish art. It was a very self-contained movement: the increase in synagogue building which was part of it went hand in hand with an upsurge of painting.

That upsurge begins with the Würzburg Biblical commentary of 1233, produced in Munich. The miniatures in this work stand isolated in the text, their style and narrative manner so precisely those of all German book illumination of the same period that in this case I do not think the painter was Jewish, although of course the possibility cannot be excluded.

FIG. 133 Jewish Minnebild (picture in the tradition of courtly love).
From the Machzor in Leipzig University Library.

The fact that the Old Testament figures depicted wear the mediaeval Jewish cap does not settle the question. One feels a natural aversion to the idea that a Jewish painter would depict this demeaning sign himself, but at this early period it still appears everywhere simply as an attribute, a distinguishing feature. A Machzor of not much later, in Leipzig, has a few sparse illustrations of the ritual of betrothal ceremonies, prayer, etc. (fig. 133). In this work the Jews do not wear the Jewish cap, but their physiological features are so strongly emphasized that at first sight they might be taken for caricatures, although such a thing is out of the question in a Jewish prayer book. It was simply seen as realism at the time.

Jewish book illumination in Germany really begins with the Machzor in the Raschi synagogue in Worms of 1272 (fig. 134). Its style is still very ornamental. Arches still of an almost Romanesque style are part of the decorative framework to the text, while animals such as lions and elephants act as bases to the lateral columns. However, Gothic turrets and naturalistic foliage are already present, along with ideas of a mystical

FIG. 134 Page from the Worms Machzor, 1272.

nature. There are figures with banderoles bearing words and mysterious symbols which are certainly Jewish, like the painter's own hand. The handwriting is rather crude and stylistically unsophisticated, something quite usual in the ghetto, which was not in close touch with the great artistic currents of the period. The wish of a Jew of the time was to be pious, not up to date.

Some twenty years later, however, in 1295/96, Nathan ben Simeon Halevy in Cologne was already producing a copy of Maimonides for his brother-in-law, a Mishnah Torah with Gothic miniatures and *drôleries*. The pages bearing ornamental letters are very fine and life-like, and the little pictures distinctly modern in the spirit of the time. However, they are few and far between, constituting painted marginal notes rather than illustrations – for instance the sacrifice of Abraham in the Book of Purities – and it seems that a Jewish painter was absolutely necessary only for the pages with the ornamental letters.

The artistic impulses of German Jewry do not make themselves felt again until we come to a fourteenth-century manuscript, a Machzor from the former Kaufmann Collection, which must have been copied shortly after 1322. Again, this book is only sparsely illustrated. It contains almost five hundred leaves, i.e. a thousand pages, but there are only twenty-two pictures, including the initials. However, these pictures are of a visionary power and mystical depth that seems to have been unknown in Jewry in any other country. The manuscript is certainly the most striking work of Jewish art in the Middle Ages, its most powerful confession of faith.

The vision preceding the text of the Song of Songs is of truly apocalyptic stature (fig. 135). King Solomon sits on his throne, wearing a red cloak. His attitude and costume are those of the time, he is sitting in a typical position, one leg crossed over the other, and is surrounded by all the grandeur of the world, for it was all subject and obedient to him – such is the tenor of the entire narrative. The canopy of his throne consists of lions and eagles. Animals of every kind crouch on the steps – mammals on the three lower steps, birds on the three upper steps. The sun, moon and stars are shown around him. The foreposts of the throne, however, show that faith is his shield: a small Torah scroll protects the right post, and a lamp, the symbol of light, the left one. In front of the king, strange creatures make their way through the letters. A dragon crawls towards the steps of the throne on human hands, followed by two men with mocking animal heads. Above them a juggler is plying his trade, a monster beating a drum rides a bird with a the horned head of a king, and two animal-human hybrids follow them. The Jewish painter has made something extraordinary of the *drôleries* of the French manuscripts. There, they were a graceful visual game, ingeniously devised; here they turn to

FIG. 135 Solomon in all his glory, painting in the Machzor of the former Kaufmann Collection, Budapest.

a horrific vision of thronging monsters. While the Christian manuscripts of the time make even the Revelation of St John the occasion for elegant painting, ideas of eternity taken from world mythology surface in this Jewish example. These weird creatures recur in all the miniatures of the book; in forms that are ever new, the painter is releasing primeval fears in his visions. No wonder the pictures showing the months provide a whole series of illustrations in this manuscript. We see not only the signs of the zodiac, frame connecting with frame, but the occupations under their influence, including some curiosities such as dog-headed twins holding a symbol of unknown significance, and Frau Minne beside them with a falcon on her hand. In general, however, the pictures show the typical occupations proper to each month: a man mowing under the sign of the Lion, harvesting under the sign of the Virgin, the vintage and the pressing of grapes under the Scorpion. The book must have had a French model; its elegance shows through very clearly in such figures as the sign of the Virgin. The one real change is that pig-killing in November is replaced by the slaughtering of sheep. However, this is the only cycle of illustrations that seems so dependent on existing models. On another page, when two armed knights on horseback are fighting, swords drawn back to strike, one is grasping the other's throat, and it is a real fight rather than a tournament (fig. 136). The Bavarian and Austrian coats of arms on the surcloths of their horses even indicate a particular battle at Mühldorf in 1322, although the picture certainly has mystic meaning.

This curious clothing of mystical ideas in the garment of reality is perceptible from now on in almost all the manuscripts created by German Jews. The strangest work of all is a Haggadah in Nuremberg dating from 1492 (fig. 137). Its pictures are nothing like what we usually think of as painted book illumination. They are not even actually painted, but are created with spaces left blank on a dark sepia background, so that they stand out light against the brown surface. Equally strange and very ambiguous are the miniatures. The pictures of the signs of the zodiac show an original imagination at work making independent use of traditional material. The archer is aiming at the goat in the next field, the water-carrier is emptying a bucket drawn from a well, and there are three

FIG. 136 Decorative page in the Machzor of the former Kaufmann Collection, Budapest.

FIG. 137 Decorative page from the Haggadah of 1492 in the
Teutonic National Museum, Nuremberg.

fishes with their heads entangled. It is all very effective, but also very
odd. Even more curious are the decorative pages. In the first place a circular
frame, probably intended to keep reminding readers of the matzos,
determines almost all the compositions as a whole and their details.
Furthermore, the sacred and the apparently secular stand side by side: the
stories of the Fall and Jonah and the Whale rub shoulders with mounted
huntsmen, and love scenes occupy the corners of the same page which
shows the Judgement of Solomon and Esau hunting. All this must have

203

FIG. 138 Pharaoh and his host ride out, from a Northern French Haggadah.
Manuscript in Manchester.

meant more than playfulness on the part of the painter.

Most German manuscripts of around 1500, however, are very different, with a distinct character of their own. They avoid self-contained composition and illustrate the text with small individual pictures and figures. The most interesting manuscripts of this type are in the libraries of Nuremberg, Hamburg and Darmstadt. Their folkloric power is reminiscent of the work of cartographers of the time, some of whom are known to have been Jewish. They are certainly of German origin. However, there are two other manuscripts of the same kind in Paris and Manchester, their approach and style suggesting that they are from the northern French or Burgundian area (fig. 138). The historical importance to art of that area is well known; its influence extended to the lower Rhine. It is not impossible that the real origins of this valuable group of manuscripts are to be sought there.

The whole spirit of the ghetto comes to life in this group of German manuscripts. Ideas, legends and history play around the text in many little pictures. The childlike and the tragic, the delicate and the robust, the commonplace and the ingenious stand side by side. It is all completely different from the contemporary pictures of Italian Jewry, which concentrated on nothing but the essentials of religious ideas. That criticism certainly cannot not be made of the painters in the German ghettos. They neither choose their subjects nor arrange them in line with any internal viewpoint, simply inserting their pictorial ideas into the words of the text. And since the text itself is sacred, they accompany it with down-to-earth verse of their own. Banderoles containing rhymed couplets are displayed beside, under and over the little pictures, explaining what is going on, making jokes, commenting. In the Italian Haggadah, the baking of the matzos was shown in three distinct separate scenes (fig. 121). The German equivalent requires twenty little pictures on four pages before it finally reaches the Seder table (fig. 139). But how charmingly, with what genuine childlike pleasure in the feast is the story told! Starting with the windmill to which the donkey has carried the grain for flour, the series runs through all the little details of preparation. Different pictures show the sack with the Passover flour being opened, the housewife tipping

FIG. 139 Baking the matzos, from the second Haggadah of the
Teutonic National Museum, Nuremberg.

FIG. 140 The Wise Man. Moses takes the crown from Pharaoh's head.
From the second Haggadah of the
Teutonic National Museum, Nuremberg.

F<small>IG</small>. 141 The Evil One. Return of the young Moses.
From the second Haggadah of the
Teutonic National Museum, Nuremberg.

flour into her bowl, kneading it, water being drawn, taken to the flour and poured in, the matzos being shaped, baked and taken out of the oven. Each of these preparations was important in the little world of the German Jew, so the verses mention the Talmudic passage prescribing a particular way of cleansing any traces of fermentation away, explain just why only the upper and lower row of barrels in the cellar are investigated, and why there is no need to look in the yard at all. Legends and fairy tales that had grown up over the centuries are woven into the story of the Exodus, and Moses has a whole new set of stories to his name. His call by God is enriched by scenes in which he takes the crown from Pharaoh's head (fig. 140); he is king of Ethiopia for forty years before being imprisoned and then rescued by his wife. The prophet Elijah, expected to appear at the Passover feast as redeemer, looks as if he came out of a child's picture book. On one occasion he appears as a knight, brandishing a large sword and riding a donkey while an angel leads it by the bridle. A procession of Jews is clinging to the animal's tail and being carried along with it. The last figure in the line is still holding half a matzo and has come straight from the Seder table. These are strange fancies in which to clothe the wishes of an oppressed people. Elsewhere, hatred of oppressors is vigorously expressed. Pharaoh is shown bathed in the blood of Israelite children, and the artist clearly relishes the painful plagues of Egypt. The Evil One (and the four types of the four questioners have a very interesting formal history) wears the clothes and carries the weapons of a warrior (fig. 141). A Machzor written by Isaak ben Simchah Gansman in 1434 contains terrible pictures of all the torments inflicted on Jews at the time, fantasies of horror woven above a dreadful reality. Nothing in the whole history of art was ever so obviously painted to give a tormented soul release as this book. Even when happy pictures or cheerful verses occasionally intervene, one cannot help feeling that they are only moments of relief in the lives of the unfortunate.

Matters reached the point where Jews in the east danced and played music at Purim or at weddings not because they felt happy but because it was legally permitted, and the permission was as good as an order. As an artistic consequence, the only book now illustrated with paintings was

FIG. 142 Consecration of the Portuguese synagogue in Amsterdam,
engraving by R. Picart. Original in the possession of the author.

the scroll of Esther, the Megillah, and eventually painters were copying
their pictures from editions illustrated with engravings.

The feeling in Sephardi and Ashkenazi art and culture was thus very
different. We cannot say now whether it arose from racial difference or
the difference in historical destiny. Too little is known of the way the
distinction between the two Jewish groups arose at all: whether the reason
was physiological or psychological. I for one am sure it was the latter.
This survey of the history of Jewish art has already shown that its cultural
links with or division from its environment were vitally important. It
cannot be denied that a racial difference existed, but cultural attitudes
decided whether Jewish art would be independent or dependent,
sophisticated or rustic. Like the art itself, the community that created it
was intellectually either free or bound. The difference between the position

of the Jews in the Islamic countries and Spain in the Middle Ages and their position in Germany was so enormous that it alone would have sufficed to produce cultural and artistic opposites.

Again, it was the Sephardic communities who retained their old outlook and culture. After being expelled from Spain they formed large communities further north, particularly in Holland and London, and during the seventeenth century these were probably the most brilliant in all Jewry. They were living in free countries and could feel secure. Surprisingly enough, however, Jewish art did not benefit much. The great synagogue of the Portuguese community in Amsterdam, considered something of a wonder (it was depicted in engravings at least three times, and was painted by the famous Dutch interior painter de Witte), was built not by a Jew but by Elias Boumann in 1675 (fig. 142). Of course, it is still Jewish in character. It was, after all, the successor to the synagogue of 1639 in which Uriel Acosta and Baruch Spinoza had been cursed. Its vaulting obviously avoids the form of the cross intentionally; the roof is barrel vaulting throughout, and conspicuously lacking in ornamentation. However, this rich community surrounded itself with all the luxury the time could afford. We may have only the gravestones in its cemetery as visible evidence, but they are sculptural works of the greatest perfection, going hand in hand with the community's history from the beginning of the seventeenth century to the middle of the eighteenth.

They follow stylistic developments in Holland very closely. Unlike the German gravestones of the time, which stand upright at the head of the grave or sarcophagus, the Sephardi monuments are slabs. The oldest of them, carved in 1614 for a dead child, is nothing but a slab bearing a finely executed inscription (fig. 143). This form seems to have remained unchanged until the middle of the seventeenth century. After the 1650s, however, richer ornamentation is found (fig. 144). At first the inscription itself remains the main motif, but it is now surrounded by decorative tendrils and symbols of a very general nature. They are not exclusively Jewish, and include the lamp, the hourglass, the skull and crossbones and once, on a doctor's gravestone, an open book. This community either did not know or did not use even the seven-branched candelabrum and star

בה

תחת העפר התפלטתי

בעיר ימים עולם נטשתי

חנוכת בית החיים עשתי

שער לפק עדן הלכתי

יוסף שמי אשר עזבתי

בן לדוד שניאור כשתי

כזאת קבר קברנ

אתי

חדש אייר יומו

שני

FIG. 143 Gravestone of Joseph, son of David Senior
(d. 11 April 1614).

FIG. 144 Gravestone of Chacham Isaac Abuab da Fonseca
(d. 4 April 1693).

FIG. 145 Gravestone of Rachel Senior Teixeira
(d. 6 March 1716).

of David, itself the symbol of the Kohanim and the Levites. On the other hand, every gravestone shows the family coat of arms: these people had retained a great deal of Spanish pride.

The outlook which emphasized Jewish origins only in the Hebrew inscription brought actual funerary sculpture at the end of the seventeenth century. The oldest gravestone with Old Testament reliefs, scenes from the stories of Abraham and David, is of 1687, while the others are all eighteenth-century. At the time, gravestones carved with figures seem to have been the rule among all the richer families and presumably gave no offence to anyone. All the scenes shown are of course from the Old Testament; even the learned allegories of antiquity, generally standard motifs at this period, were carefully avoided. The scenes include the three angels visiting Abraham, the appearance of God to Samuel before the ark of the covenant (God is actually depicted, making this probably the most daring of all Jewish monuments), and the death of Rachel, on the tomb of a lady also called Rachel who like her matriarchal namesake died in childbirth (fig. 145). All these sculptural works relate to the personal histories of the dead, and the names of the Old Testament characters they show are those of the people buried in the graves. On the other hand, the coat of arms is now omitted, while mourning angels and similar figures are found in profusion. Obviously the Spanish Jews of Holland had become increasingly a part of their surroundings. These are manifestations of assimilation, of a kind also found in Germany at the end of the eighteenth century

Similarly, some very gifted Jewish painters of portrait miniatures lived in England in the seventeenth century. Miniature painting was a very popular art of great social significance; cultivated society particularly valued these little pictures because of their elegance. For an artistically talented Jew barred on religious grounds from painting on a larger scale, they were virtually a refuge. The two Cooper brothers were the most famous of these painters, and since their teacher John Hoskins, even more distinguished in holding the position of court painter, is described as their uncle, he may have been Jewish too. Of the two Coopers, Samuel (1609–1672) was the more important, and was a popular painter during

Cromwell's rule and later at the court of Charles II. His grave style has genuine quality and the ability to convey his subjects' individuality. In the tradition of Van Dyck, he paints miniature portraits without the conventional sentimentality to which the elegance of the genre so easily seduced artists. Like so many Jews who became successful, Samuel Cooper later abjured his faith. His brother Alexander, who was four years older, was successful in northern parts of Europe, particularly Sweden.

The Ashkenazi Jews of Germany and Poland were the greatest possible contrast to this aristocratic community that had its coats of arms, its envoys, negotiated with princes and traded in the Orient and North Africa. It is the same contrast we found expressed in art, a contrast between an oppressed and a free intellectual world, a life lived under constraints or a life at liberty. The Middle Ages were not over for the Ashkenazi Jews, in their position in society as well as other fields, and there were not even any external reasons for the situation. In the kingdom of Poland they had a great deal of personal freedom, their own administration and their own law court; they formed their own section of society, and as merchants and craftsmen they were socially a class above the peasants. However, Poland itself had no sophisticated culture, and so this freedom was of very relative value. Art received no new stimulus such as it had been given in the Middle Ages. In addition, the intellectual world of eastern Judaism was increasingly determined by doctrinal schools and their rabbinical atmosphere, where exegesis rather than creative ideas ruled. The value set on this kind of scholarship forced artistic interests in general into the background. The spirit of the Jewish east had turned too far away from the world to think much of art.

Art therefore became rustic, assuming the character of robust folk art. We no longer feel that such art is inferior; on the contrary, all countries of the present day are aware of the strength residing in these links with the land and its plain way of life. Those links were certainly present among Polish Jews in particular. They were not, like the German Jews, forced to confine themselves to trade, but were primarily craftsmen, and indeed the backbone of Polish crafts. They were organized into guilds; the Jewish tailors' guild of Kurnik, for instance, had forty-four members in the year 1754, and held divine service in its own guild chamber. Such guild chambers can still be seen in a number of synagogues. Here the contrast with conditions in Germany verges on the grotesque. In his residence of Dresden, the same king in whole Polish domains Jewish craftsmen were taken for granted had difficulty in obtaining admission to the goldsmiths' guild for his court goldsmith Rachel, whose father had converted from the faith.

There were genuine Jewish crafts and genuine Jewish art in Poland, then; art was not simply put to the service of the synagogues and Jewish buildings. Among ten thousand Jewish craftsmen in sixteenth-century Poland, the largest number were workers in the textile industry and furriers, and next come the goldsmiths. It is natural enough for them to be near the top of the list of craftsmen, since ornaments and expensive vessels were almost the only way of adorning the house of God richly. However, we also know of Jewish architects such as Hillel Benjamin, who built the synagogues of Kurnik and Lutomiersk in 1767 and fell to his death during the building of another synagogue in Zloczow, and the woodcarver Samuel Goldbaum, who carved the doors of the Torah ark in Kempen and then moved to Bydgoscz (Bromberg). There is no doubt that everything Jewish in the east was really made by Jews; they were the only people in the country capable of doing it.

The path taken by Jewish art up to this point can be very easily traced. It led from west to east, from Germany to Poland. This accounts for the relationship between the Altneuschule in Prague and the Gothic synagogue in Cracow. And just as the Yiddish language originates in the German Middle Ages, many shapes of utensils are German in origin. The spice box has two basic shapes, found in many variations: it is shaped like a pear or like a tower. Both designs had their roots in the art of German goldsmiths of the late Gothic period, around 1500, and must have gone eastward with it. As early as about 1600, however, the craftsmanship of the east was clearly superior. Even Prague had nothing more to offer it. A Jewish architect died in that city in 1625; his name, Juda Goldschmied de Herz, suggests that he began his career as a goldsmith, and his gravestone tells us that he built the Pinkas synagogue and a part of the Meisl

FIG. 146 Cemetery of the Prague community.

synagogue. Although these buildings are no smaller than the Altneuschule they are by no means such a fine achievement. They lack the crucial element of artistic assurance. The synthesis between Gothic tradition and individual Italian forms which had long since become the modern approach has not been attained, and while that discrepancy runs right through the contemporary art of the north, these synagogues entirely lack the presence we sense in the Gothic synagogue of Prague. However, Prague was still the western city of the greatest importance to Jewish art. The gravestones of its cemetery are perhaps the best counterparts to the Sephardi gravestones of the Amsterdam community (fig. 146). These monuments are characteristic of Ashkenazi austerity, tolerating no real sculptural features, only plain frames, but fortunately making much use of Jewish symbols. After the middle of the seventeenth century, when the area had recovered from the damage inflicted by the Thirty Years' War, there was even something like a new flowering of art. The finest of the gravestones were erected at this period, and most important of all the Jewish Rathaus, the outward sign of self-administration, was built. Ferdinand III gave permission for its construction in 1645. It was burnt down twice; today it stands next to the Gothic synagogue, an impressive sight (fig. 125). The present building was constructed in 1765 by Joseph Schlesinger from Breslau, an architect in great demand, and it is a typical work of the Baroque architecture that has left such a mark on the face of Prague. Sturdy pilasters stand at the corners of the building as if to support it. The arches over the windows provide emphatic accents. The roof is a plain hipped roof with oriel windows, and the symbol of the Jewish religion stands confidently on top of the clock tower. However, Prague is a unique case, for it had an old-established Jewish community with special privileges.

The emphasis had now moved entirely to Poland, where the art of synagogue building became creative and developed a new type of monument. The synagogue of Isaak Nachmanowicz (ben Nachman) in Lemberg, built in 1582, is the last to employ Gothic vaulting, and displays Renaissance style only in its ornamental details. However, it is far superior to the Pinkas synagogue in Prague, and gives the impression of being very carefully designed. On the other hand, the Polish synagogues of the seventeenth century bear the stamp of the new Baroque period, while at the same time being very independent. A new style did not reach these remote areas at first hand, in the same way as it came to Venice or Amsterdam. Here in Poland it was more robust, the walls sturdier, the ground plan laid out to individual requirements and not as a copy of some famous church. The focal point is still the almemar. However, while it was fitted between the pillars dividing the building into two area in the Gothic synagogues, there is now a genuinely centralized layout. The Lemberg synagogue of 1632, on the outskirts of the town, is an almost square hall with four central octagonal pillars and the almemar in the middle. Wall arches proceeding from the pillars bear up the vault. An architectonic walk around the whole building leads to offices and guild chambers, and on the upper storey the women's galleries look down on the main area. The men's and women's synagogues are therefore arranged as the main room and an annexe to it. The whole building is a unified structure containing all the rooms required for the congregation's needs, a centre for the whole community. Besides providing places for the almemar and the Torah ark, the Polish synagogues now have a new site incorporated in the building for the niche with the eternal light.

This type of building remained the standard for the great synagogues of Poland. In the synagogue of Zolkiew (built after 1692), the two synagogues of Rzeszow and the synagogues of Przewrosk and Przemysl, the latter being perhaps the oldest, only one alteration is noticeable: the four central pillars are in increasingly close proximity to the reader's desk, drawing further and further together and concentrating the building around its centre. On the outside, too, the impression is monumental and marked by the energy that, wrongly, is not usually ascribed to Jews. These synagogues were built like citadels, centres of resistance in a country full of unrest. Outwards, they look like solid blocks. The building, supported by massive flying buttresses, resembles a squat tower with solid battlements and loopholes. It was important for the community of Prague, and for many other communities, to be able to defend itself.

In the eighteenth century Polish synagogues became rustic, like their

FIG. 147 Façade of the wooden synagogue, Zabludowo.

congregations. This was probably as a result of the heavy debts they had incurred; in the year 1717 the debts of Polish Jewry amounted to 280,000 Polish guilders, and fifty years later it was over a million. At the time the whole country was in economic decline, and the contrast between the rich nobility and the destitute citizens and peasants was particularly marked in Poland. However, one cannot call these rustic wooden synagogues inferior. In a Slav country with its own style of wooden architecture they may even be seen as more important than their stone-built counterparts, having more of a character of their own. They were contemporary with the urban type, and have their own history. The oldest, those of the seventeenth century, like the synagogues of Zabludowo (fig. 147) and Nasielsk – the name of the Jewish architect there is known – are the richest, most original and most stylistically imaginative. Their outward appearance is almost fantastic. The roof, raised like a tower, dominates the building, but in many different variants. Level by level, curving out, hipped, dipping down again, it rises in grand outline to the rooftree.

221

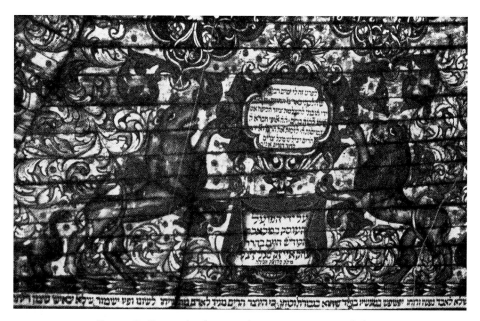

FIG. 148 Fresco in the wooden synagogue, Mohilew.

Oriels and annexes make the silhouette of the whole building remarkably attractive. The wooden balustrades and pillars are carved in such detail that their movement seems almost restless. The style does not calm down until the onset of classicism at the end of the eighteenth century, as in the synagogue of Kurnik, built by the master Hillel Benjamin in 1767. This building has a simple centralized plan, with plain wooden walls of no great interest on the outside, and a plain roof in only two sections. The portal, again, is only an imitation of the western forms that had long been dominant in contemporary Poland, and the murals inside the building consist of static garlands in the style of the period. In the seventeenth century, wall painting had been so lively and attractive that the walls and wooden ceilings of many synagogues were almost entirely covered with its imaginative creations (fig. 148). Chodorow was painted in this way in 1642, Jablonow in 1674, and we even know the name of the painter in Mohilew – Isaak Eisik Segal. It is as if the wild imagination of the late Gothic German Haggadahs had become even more exaggerated here. The human figure is of course usually avoided, and Biblical scenes are

FIG. 149 The wooden synagogue of Kirchheim. Würzburg,
the Luitpold Museum.

rare but not unknown. Animals and plants predominate, but in what variety! Besides the animals of Ezekiel's prophetic vision there are parrots, snakes, camels, the pelican, the cockerel and indeed every possible creature that could be taken as symbolic. The lion was of course especially popular. Landscape features are particularly frequent in Mohilew, where a fantastic view of Worms with a dragon in front of it perhaps refers to some tradition derived from the Nibelungenlied which went east with the language. The tendrils between these scenes proliferate fantastically in so wild and attractive a manner that a possible origin for the style in Armenia has been suggested, although it is probably only a matter of Baroque forms being enlivened by eastern influence. The colours are bright and striking, with strong contrasts set side by side. Ornamentation of the few other items still open to Jewish painters once printing had become the main means of book manufacture, such as the *kethuba* (the marriage contract) and the *misrach* panel (showing the direction of prayer) is in the same style, showing imagination beating against the strongest barriers ever set against it by religious precept.

Curiously enough, the wooden synagogues of Poland have counterparts in the area of the river Main in Germany. These are the synagogues of Horb (now transferred to the museum in Bamberg), Kirchheim (now in Würzburg Museum) (fig. 149), Bechhofen, etc. They are small and modest; large prayer houses were not permitted. Instead, they were richly painted, and it has been suggested that the type derives from Poland in a kind of process of reverse emigration. However, the points of coincidence are very slight, and are really confined to the fact that these synagogues too were painted and were made of wood inside. On the outside, they were plain half-timbered buildings of the typical Franconian kind. The ground plan is not central either, but is to a rectangular design, expressed in particular in the vaulting, with a long barrel vault going down the middle and flat ceilings at the sides. I found the same kind of vaulting in the synagogue of the old ghetto of Tüchersfeld in Franconian Switzerland, which is extremely well preserved and very little known.

In fact the paintings of the Franconian synagogues diverge so much from the Polish examples that we may say they are in a completely different style. It is one which relies heavily on tendrils; there are certainly a great many animals among them, but they never predominate as they do further east. The tendril patterns themselves are very like the pomegranate and rose patterns of the late Gothic period in southern Germany. At least in one case, the Kirchheim synagogue, we know who the painter was; he describes himself as Lazarus Susman, son of Salomo, cantor of Brod, and therefore came from Bohemia. His work is much finer and more sophisticated than anything produced in Poland.

There were now quite precisely determined shapes for Jewish cultic utensils, the same basic elements being retained, although with some or even with considerable variation. First among the Torah ornaments were the ribbons binding the parchment scrolls themselves. They were often presented by families on the occasion of their sons' bar mitzvahs, and were usually embroidered, genuine works of domestic craftsmanship and in the tradition of folk art. The mantle of the Torah bears expensive gold embroidery, often on velvet from the time of the Baroque period. The design of the embroidery is usually non-yurative, showing only tendrils, crowns, or the tables of the law. This last motif occurs again on the silver shield hung around the scroll as a breast ornament. Its design is richer: typical motifs are an arch containing the tables of the law, or two lions holding a crown as on a coat of arms. Such motifs were the most frequently used in general, and also occur, for instance, on the outer curtain of the holy ark. The two coronals may be in the shape of little towers or worked together as a crown, and have little bells hanging in them. Representing an elongation of the hand as it does, the pointer logically enough has the shape of a pointing hand at its tip. These silverware items followed the development of style up to the Rococo period and into the present day. Countless old examples from every century survive, but they are almost always the work of Christian master silversmiths. They become increasingly important with the increase in veneration of the Torah as the tangible, present object of instruction.

It is characteristic of Judaism, however, that heightened effectiveness is seen as residing in sobriety rather than brilliance. While a Gothic winged altar shows its sober exterior on working days, and is opened on festival days to show the gilded carving within, it was exactly the other way round in the synagogue. The curtain bore coloured embroidery on weekdays, but on the greatest festival days it was white and perfectly plain, and the closer any item comes to the scroll itself the less ornamentation it ventures to bear. The old, awed feeling that art was not serious and the holy of holies would not tolerate its proximity runs like a law through all the centuries of Jewish art.

CHAPTER FIVE

The Way to the Present Day

ALL AT once, innumerable artistic talents awoke in Israel, as if storming all the barriers. From the end of the eighteenth century, Jewish name follows Jewish name in the history of art in unbroken succession, some great names above them, pioneers who did not lack followers. Relatively speaking, the number of Jewish artists is extraordinarily high. Only now does it become evident that Israel was as gifted as any other people for the freedom of great art, and only external causes had prevented those gifts from unfolding earlier. Once Jewish artists left the ghetto and the Jewish community to enter the world and compete for general recognition they had to prove their worth, and so indeed they did.

The right to this achievement was not won without a struggle; few rights are. After the time of Voltaire and Lessing, however, at least the struggle was not for the mere right to exist. Israel's aim was first to be regarded as human among other human beings, then to be a nation among other nations. The first steps taken in that direction were a consequence more of the dawning of social understanding than of pure humanity. As soon as the world recognized that there were no special classes of people, the aristocracy and the upper classes, who had special rights from birth, the Jews could no longer be regarded as belonging to a low caste, and it would have looked strange to emancipate black people while tolerating exceptive laws for members of a white race in Europe itself. The way from this realization to putting it into practice, however, was a very long one, and if the truth be told, it has not yet reached its end.

FIG. 150 The synagogue in the Heidereutergasse, Berlin, from an engraving.

For Jewish art, emancipation meant that Jews at last had the opportunity for free existence and creativity. The lifting of the bans that had forced Jewish worship in Germany into small prayer rooms made it possible to design large synagogues again. Fine places of worship were built in the second half of the eighteenth century, with great zeal, but there was no tradition to call upon, and without exception, so far as is known, Christian architects had to be commissioned to construct these buildings. Berlin was granted royal permission to build the great synagogue in the Heidereutergasse as early as 1712 (fig. 150). This was a single large hall with high windows and a barrel vault, a form known at the time as Gothic. The palace chapel in Versailles was described by the same term. In fact the style is Baroque, and the ark for the Torah scrolls is constructed like a two-storey altar. The almemar still stands in the middle, an arrangement not abandoned until the nineteenth century.

The most important synagogues of the eighteenth century were built in its second half, and thus, in north-west Bohemia where the nobility were particularly unprejudiced and had lively intellectual interests, they were in the Rococo style. The finest was in Kuttenplan, completed in 1759. It is very impressive with its four majestic double pilasters, great arches soaring up from them through the main axis of the cupola. Graceful Rococo stucco work relieves the massivity of the design. However, the only Jewish thing about it is the centralized layout and the use of purely ornamental decoration in a style which otherwise always included figures. Both the dangers and the great opportunities that emancipation entailed for the development of Judaism and Jewish art are expressed in these buildings. The forms of the time are employed, but Jewish creativity was not at first strong enough to control them.

The same problem faced the Jewish artist – or rather, the artistically gifted Jew of the time. Where he might previously have suppressed his talents, or kept them within the narrow limits offered in the community, he now understandably wanted to bring the achievement of which he felt capable to completion. Of its very nature, the age of the Enlightenment was intellectually dominated, with the emphasis on rationality and understanding. The Jew stepped purposefully out into a strange world where he claimed the same rights as everyone else, and still he encountered barriers, prejudices and exceptive laws. As a Jew, he had no professional future. It was difficult for him to bring his work before the public. He had no chance to earn good money or take long journeys. Many institutes of art education were closed to him. He therefore faced the choice of abandoning the attempt or converting, and often chose the latter course.

For the ties binding him to the Jewish tradition had worn thin. The world of the Enlightenment that had liberated him, and that he loved, was unwilling to believe in what it could not see. Its leaders, like Voltaire, were anti-clerical, even atheistic. Religious commitment seemed to them unimportant or without foundation. Modern Jewish art, then, unfortunately begins with no Jewish artists but a number of converts. However, they deserve mention, not only because conversion may deny community but does not abolish it, but because the phenomenon itself is characteristic of the history of Jewish art.

The first step was taken during the eighteenth century. The artists involved were mostly gifted Jewish painters of miniatures, and the circle of co-religionists for whom they could work was too small for them. They entered the service of the courts, frequently changing their faith in the process. Their names include Joseph Marquard Treu of Bamberg (1712–1796, Joel Nathan before his baptism), whose son Johann Nikolaus Treu became one of the most popular altar painters of Franconia; Juda Pinhas (1727–1793) who began his career as a Megillah painter before taking service at the court of a margrave, and whose descendants were artists for two generations; the miniature painter Jeremias David Alexander Fiorino (1793–1847), born in Kassel and active at the court of Dresden, and finally the most interesting of them all, Ismael Mengs (1690–1746), who came from Bohemia, converted to Christianity and painted miniatures and enamels, and whose Catholic son, the famous Anton Raffael Mengs, was the favourite painter of the courts of Dresden, Madrid and many other capitals. His talents are unquestioned – he was the creator of an abstract style of religious painting which was of great significance for ecclesiastical art. The path taken by the Mengs family is thus very typical: the father first enters the new circle as a miniature painter, the son is almost always found working for the church.

However, art is not to be produced at will: it is strong only when it is compulsive. The Jew who entered the world of great ecclesiastical art saw it more as a means to an end than an end in itself. It was not art that inspired him but ambition and determination, and for that very reason he failed to scale the heights. These artists were typically able to turn their hands to anything, but they were not outstanding.

The next generation faced complex problems. They had to do more than take the first step over the divide, they had to settle into the new world beyond it. Life all around them had changed. Rationalism, that almost primitive form of thinking whose strength lay in conflict rather than construction, had fulfilled its historical duty. As always, and as we still see today, the next generation was intellectually ready and indeed eager for spiritual experience. The spirit of Klopstock triumphed over the spirit of Lessing. A desire for piety and religion set in more strongly then ever, and Romanticism was born. It clung to the naïve faith of the Middle Ages. It wanted to be Gothic, to be religious, in the process retreating further and further from real life, becoming ever more abstract and bloodless.

Those Jews who had already left their own sphere far enough behind to be influenced by this movement still saw it only at second hand. Far from seeking mystical experience in their own religion, they were swept away by the piety of the Christian Middle Ages. At least the very numerous conversions to Catholicism of the early nineteenth century cannot now be attributed to cold opportunism, but those lost to Judaism in the process were all the more valuable.

In the world of art, they included Philipp Veit, born in Berlin in 1793. His mother Dorothea converted to Catholicism with him and his brother. She was a daughter of Moses Mendelssohn, and her second marriage was to the mystic Friedrich Schlegel. At the time of his conversion Philipp Veit was ten years old. It was typical that the family's baptism, the outcome of feeling and spiritual emotion rather than conviction, was in the choir of Cologne Cathedral. In 1815 Veit joined the so-called Nazarene artists

FIG. 151 Eduard Bendemann, *The Mourning Jews in Babylon.*
Cologne, the Museum.

in Rome; the group included Overbeck and Cornelius. He worked with them on painting the story of Joseph in the Casa Bartoldy. Later, as director of the Städel Art Institute in Frankfurt, his works showed almost exclusively New Testament scenes. His last paintings were the frescos in the dome of Mainz Cathedral; he died in Mainz in 1877. If we compare him with, for instance, Cornelius, it is clear that he is more the man of feeling but a lesser painter. Cornelius was an artist who sought expression in religious painting. Veit was carried away by the mystical current of the time and sought to provide it with art. The difference is fundamental. Veit's art is acquired rather than experienced, and there is sometimes an alarming emptiness about his pictures. Characteristically, Cornelius also painted other subjects, particularly from Greek mythology, but Veit kept to religious themes.

Eduard Bendemann (1811–1889, active in Berlin and Düsseldorf, converted in 1835) is basically different from Veit in recognizing the emotional value to painting of the Jewish destiny. His pictures *The*

FIG. 152 Eduard Bendemann, *The Destruction of Jerusalem.*
Berlin, National Gallery.

Mourning Jews in Babylon (1832) (fig. 151) and *Jeremiah in the Ruins of Jerusalem*
(1837) were the first real examples of Jewish works of art of this kind
painted by a Jew. However, his aim is not the subject itself so much as its
effect on the viewer, which he assesses with great precision. He sought to
grip and overwhelm his viewers, as the painting of his time did in general,
and while he had great success with these paintings, there was something
about them rather like an exhibition of Jewish misfortunes. His work
gradually became more energetic and his style more resolute. His great
picture of 1872, *The Destruction of Jerusalem,* is a work of real historical
passion (fig. 152). Other works of his include the frescos in the state
rooms of the palace in Dresden.

The bourgeois counterpart to spectacular art of this nature was genre

FIG. 153 Moritz Oppenheim, *The Wedding*.

painting. It too aims to influence the viewer, but to move rather than overwhelm him. It looks at everyday life, finding little happiness there but many tears, and shows familiar settings with something to say to everyone. The Jewish pioneer in this field was Moritz Oppenheim (born in Hanau 1799, active in Frankfurt am Main, where he died in 1882). He bears the same relation to genre painting as Bendemann to historical painting, but is much closer to Judaism at heart. Even his famous *Return of the Volunteer* was so successful because it pointed out that the Jew was a patriot. His pictures of Jewish family life take the first step towards a conception of the Jewish world (fig. 153). The series covers the Sabbath and the festival days, the quiet contentment and cheerful peace of home, and the piety and emotion of worship. Today his style seems lifeless and empty, avoiding all expression of power and activity and seeking out life's sentimental moments. We find the idealized beauty of these Jewish people, their artificial poses, and the smooth draughtsmanship intolerable, knowing as we do how hard their lives really were. However, neither do we believe that the peasants painted by contemporary artists went hay-making every day and always had a knife ready to hand. It is not Oppenheim and Bendemann who fail to be true to life; their period believed in a contrast between art and reality, and thought the mission of art was to improve upon a reality thought to be too commonplace.

The attitude of Jewish artists of the time to synagogue building, the Jewish community's most important task, shows how they had lost touch with their roots. Academic training at the time was not much use to any budding architects, but was positively fatal if they were Jewish. The model – and this was the fault of the contemporary understanding of history, not solely expressed in historical painting – the model was seen as the classical example, and classical architecture was basically misunderstood. It had once been vigorously alive, expressing the spirit of its time. Now teachers were not encouraging their pupils to capture the spirit of their own times with equal vigour, creating buildings that would serve it just as well, but to adapt works of the past for the modern world. The result was an architectural masquerade, all the worse because it contradicted the whole meaning of architecture, which sets out to fulfil basic needs, constructing buildings where people can live their lives.

It was understandable enough for the building of churches in mediaeval styles or in imitation of St Peter's in Rome to continue. Those styles might not be of the present, but they were still ecclesiastical. What, however, was the point of building Gothic and Romanesque synagogues? Yet the hybrid mediaeval style invented by Edwin Oppler (born 1831 in Oels) was typical of nineteenth-century synagogue architecture. It swept through Germany, and Max Fleischer even built the synagogue in Budweis like a Gothic church with a façade and two towers.

It was also at least understandable for the Moorish style to be used in synagogues (there are examples in Florence and Berlin, in the synagogues of Adolf Wolff in Esslingen and Fernbach in New York). The period of Moorish rule in Spain had seen the heyday of Jewish culture. But what was their connection with the Jewish present? In any case, the outcome was usually a church ground plan in Jewish disguise, the Jewish architect having absorbed the principles of church architecture from his academic training. He might, for instance, place the almemar on the narrower wall, like an altar, failing to grasp the unsuitability of that situation in a Jewish place of worship. Only recently a synagogue was built in Germany with a domed interior, while the exterior imitates the façade of the Zeno church in Verona, which has three naves: there is a total incongruity between the façade and the ground plan which cannot be excused by the fact that it is equally ignorantly applied to churches. These synagogues are in fact typical of the spiritual culture of Israel in the nineteenth century. Magnificent buildings expressing no identity of their own, although they have failed to master any other identity, they bear witness to an internal insecurity that no amount of surface brilliance could hide.

Towards the end of the century artistic sensibility changed completely and became objective. The business of architecture was no longer to create an atmosphere but to build, and here were the foundations upon which Jewish artists could at last begin their work. The mental burdens of the ghetto were finally shed. The Jewish artist no longer had to study worlds unknown to him at first hand in order to participate fully in the culture of his time, he had only to fulfil his task. The view lay straight ahead. A great many problems and questions of outlook were simply swept aside, in a manner that was a relief to all creative artists but particularly to a Jewish architect, who was finally liberated from the pressures of history and free to tackle the tasks of present.

He was well equipped for them. At the very beginning of the movement, in Berlin, stands Alfred Messel (1853–1909), although he was only born Jewish. He did not entirely overcome his training in historical techniques. His dwelling houses in Berlin and his museum in Darmstadt still have Baroque façades, and he inclines to the Greek style in the vast designs for

FIG. 154 Erich Mendelsohn, observatory for Prof. Einstein, Potsdam.

the new buildings of the Berlin museum. But he gives a modern look to a modern commission, the Wertheim department store in Berlin. He liberates the stone and iron building from any need to conceal itself behind Baroque pilasters or in rustic disguise; he sees that a department store is a building for the sale of goods in large quantities, and no more. We can see trace Messel's increasingly clear understanding of this from plan to plan; for instance, he designed the two open-air courtyards in the Wertheim store with about a decade between them, and sculptural ornamentation has entirely disappeared from the second.

It may have been the logic of modern architecture and spatial design that made Jews particularly good at fulfilling its demands. The intention is to construct a perfectly functional building, and it is expressed in logical architectural structures. In Holland, for instance, which was to the fore

FIG. 155 Leo Nachtlicht, interior.

throughout the movement, the architect M. de Klerk of Amsterdam, who died young, created bold, clear-cut plans that did not shrink from an architectural effect of harshness, and Erich Mendelsohn (born 1887 in Allenstein) is a contemporary proponent of the style in Berlin. He stands alone amidst the throng of the talented and untalented, those with great gifts and those with fewer, the leaders and their followers who have made what amounts to a business out of functional modern art. I shall hardly be contradicted if I describe him as the most important contemporary architect in Berlin and perhaps all of Germany. His achievement, at a time when theories, opinions and fantastic notions were coming thick and fast in every country, is to have kept a clear head and found what was necessary for his task without ever creating dry, calculated designs. His buildings are always works of art wholly fulfilling their purpose. He seeks his tasks in the present. His progress is marked by the

FIGS 156 & 157 Emmy Roth, silver goblet and candelabrum.

superbly massive experimental tower for Einstein (1921) (fig. 154), his rebuilding of the Mossehaus (1923), as interesting in its approach to corners as to the relationship of wall and window, an office building in Gleiwitz (1922), factories, villas, apartment blocks and finally the layout of the amusement complex in the Lehniner Platz (1928), which is more than just a building and is characteristic of modern urban architecture in general. He must be one of the most productive and imaginative architects of the day, and one of those most conscious of his purpose, a man with an almost perfect sense of style.

However, he is not by any means the only modern Jewish architect of stature. Oskar Strnad (born 1879) has designed buildings in Vienna with a remarkable sense of grace and comfort about them. His buildings, like the reception room in the Austrian Pavilion at the Cologne Manufacturing League exhibition, or the Grinzing apartment block, are strikingly slender and airy, with very discreet ornamentation. He has had a great influence

239

on arts and crafts in Austria, an influence which is of a generally cultural nature in the same way as that of Hofmannsthal and Klimt, and which thus extends far beyond his own field into the whole direction taken by Viennese taste. In Berlin, Leo Nachtlicht is to some extent a similar case, though he is less of a leader, but he solves problems with modern means and ideas, very much in the spirit of his city. The conversion of the Sezession building, various villas, and the Gurmenia building are among Nachtlicht's larger buildings in Berlin, and his designs for the competition to build the new synagogue in the Klopstockstrasse should also be mentioned. The whole interior design of these buildings also shows Nachtlicht's gift for craftsmanship (fig. 155). It is not his alone. We could in fact wonder whether craftsmanship was not so intensively practised throughout all the centuries of the *goluss* and ghetto for the very reason that Jews are particularly gifted in art of a domestic nature. At any rate, the names of Jewish craftsmen cannot all be mentioned here simply because there are so many, and if we add, as we should, artists working for trade and industry, advertising artists, display-window dressers and fashion artists, the number becomes truly vast. Women are particularly gifted in these areas, their natural feeling for the effect of decorative features making them seem ideally suited to crafts and design. Increasingly cast on their own resources in modern life, they have found an important field of activity here. Among them at least one particularly notable name deserves mention, that of Frau Emmy Roth, whose work as a silversmith is on the borderline where craft becomes art and utensils become sculpture, losing all extraneous ornamentation and become an expression of the living present (figs 156, 157).

And that is the crucial factor – for we are not concerned with just one branch of art in this entire movement, not even one as important as architecture, but with the artistic philosophy of modern man. We are concerned with the acknowledgement of objectivity as the artist's vital task. Developments in painting since the middle of the nineteenth century, the struggle for realism, are a part of the same transformation of artistic endeavour, and Jewish artists occupy an equal place in it.

In painting, two great steps were taken: realism and impressionism.

Realism took its subjects from actuality, recognizing that the environment of real life could provide art with as much expressive material as any romantic world, a ploughman is as good a subject as a triumphant general and a ploughed field can be beautiful. This meant the end of historical painting and sentimentality. Indeed, it was a question of social insight casting light on art, and had almost direct relevance to the Jews. One is not surprised that the writer who represented this view of the world, Zola, was also the principal campaigner in the Dreyfus trial. Truth was at stake.

The second step, impressionism, which reached its peak in the 1870s, dispensed in its own turn with such subjects and with any attempt to attract the attention of the public by anything but the picture itself. It was interested not in What, but in How. It found its scope in landscape, still life and the portrait. The question was purely one of painting. Colour now reigned supreme; the sensitivity of the eye and the power of the composition were the crucial factors determining the value of the picture. At the same time there was a break with all conventions of outline and colouring. The individual view of nature was what mattered.

This was the real act of liberation in painting. It gave artists the right to be entirely independent of schools and doctrines, to be wholly themselves. You could not 'feel your way' into impressionism. You had to see, and see for yourself. This was the moment when Jewish painters really came into their own, liberating themselves along with their art.

Joseph Israels was the leading figure in Dutch realism. He was born in 1824, and his work is inconceivable without the great achievements of his French contemporary Millet, the first artist who had the courage to love and paint the work of peasants. None the less, Israels has a very individual style, in no way derivative (figs 158, 159). He loves the quiet interiors of Holland, sees – and sees better than Millet – how light flows through them from the window, gliding quietly over human figures and slowly dying away on the walls. He sees the beauty of a group of girls sitting together sewing, and the grave atmosphere of the fisherman's living room. All this is still slightly sentimental, depending on atmosphere, even if the atmosphere is one of work. But there are some pictures –

FIG. 158 Joseph Israels, *Return Home.*
By permission of the Galerie Thannhauser.

those drawn from the artist's Jewish background – which have the direct power of life. When we see a Jewish tradesman sitting outside his shop door, in the famous etching known as *The Son of the Old Nation,* he is a man waiting wearily, looking into space unthinkingly, his hands hanging heavily from his sleeves. Israels paints a Jewish wedding and shows two ordinary people for once celebrating a feast day, hardly knowing how to be happy. In such pictures his use of line is as strong as life itself. He sees quickly and with penetration, drawing every last drop of character from the incident, and its spiritual content with it. Oppenheim's poetic ghetto pictures seem lifeless by comparison. The reason for the difference lies very deep. It is not only the difference between a painter who wants to arouse feelings and one who actually has them, but the difference between a Jew of the past who still finds it rather strange to be painting Jewish subjects, and a Jew of the present who sees it as quite natural. Israels died in 1911.

Fig. 159 Joseph Israels, *Jewish Wedding.* Vienna. Private ownership.

The same impressionist generation has two Jewish painters leading the movement in the two principle impressionist countries: Camille Pissarro in France and Max Liebermann in Germany.

Camille Pissarro (1830–1903), the eldest of the entire group of painters, in fact represents a clear synthesis of their aims. French impressionism was intuitive, quick to see, experienced its subject directly and worked fast, placing strong, sunny colours on the canvas (fig. 160). He was the artistic exponent of a new temperament that had no time for quiet interiors now, but created its works out in life and the sunlight. However, Pissarro worked very systematically. In the 1860s he began painting pictures of strong structure, well constructed and very clear, in colours that were not too dazzling. Within a decade he had made his way to a freer style, observing that material objects such as houses, trees, a river, do not remain

Fig. 160 Camille Pissarro, *Le Jardin des Tuileries.*
By permission of the Galerie Thannhauser.

always the same, since the light and thus their colours change. This marks
the point in impressionism where mind overcomes matter. Pissarro loves
the play of colour in the trees, their reflections in water, the gradations
of sunlight on walls which cast it back like a mirror. For a short time, at
the beginning of the 1890s, he partook of the experiments of so-called
neo-impressionism, separating mixtures of colours into their pure, basic
tones so that they stand side by side in bright little dabs, and the picture
shimmers as if it were in the sun. In 1896. however, he was writing to
Van de Velde that he no longer considered himself part of that group,
having recognized the lifelessness of their manner of painting, which
was in essence theoretical, a method and not a natural way of seeing
things. In short, he was an extremely critical man who took a very critical
view of his own work and that of his period, and developed his ideas

logically. He was the ideal teacher of the next generation – almost all its great figures learned in Pissarro's studio. His son was also a painter, but did not attain anything like the father's independent stature.

There is an inner relationship between Pissarro, Messel, Mendelsohn and the great painter of German impressionism, Max Liebermann. It lies in that same capacity for self-criticism, this conscious development of the artist's own abilities from one achievement to the next. Liebermann became the teacher of the rising generation in Germany as Pissarro did in France. Otherwise, however, he is as far removed from Pissarro as a German can be from a French artist. If anyone needs proof that during periods of assimilation culture can have more influence than race, then the antithesis of these two masters provides it.

Max Liebermann, born in 1847, came from an old mercantile family in Berlin (fig. 161). Characteristically, he was not originally drawn to the impressionists; his orientation was determined by Holland and the Barbizon school. He began his career at the age of twenty-seven, with the *Women Plucking Geese*. The meaning of the work resides in the way the subject is seen, in the movement of the figures in harsh lighting. It picks out the gestures and characterful faces of the old women working against the dark background. The picture is almost entirely dark; light comes into Liebermann's work in 1881 with the *Cobbler's Workshop*. The artist has now entirely mastered the way it fills the interior and is thrown back from the walls to give a sense of airiness and perspective. The people shown at work are more peaceful, seated more naturally at the cobbler's bench. The artist is in better control of his material; there is no sense of artificial posing now. Liebermann was mastering landscape at this time, a more difficult achievement, for light glides less easily off landscape structures and provides stronger, more dazzling illumination. However, he acquired this technique as well: in the 1870s Liebermann's landscapes are entirely spatial, and human figures occupy them as confidently as they do his interiors. His landscapes reach their peak with *The Woman with the Goats* (fig. 162). It is a depiction of labour rendered without sentimentality or pathos, showing only an old woman making her way home through the dunes and leading a goat on a halter. However, the

FIG. 161 Max Liebermann, *Self-Portrait*, 1926.
By permission of the publishing firm of Bruno Cassirer, Berlin.

FIG. 162 Max Liebermann, *The Woman with the Goats*, 1890.
Munich, the Pinakothek.

movement which dominates the picture, the tension of the woman's arm
and her bent neck, give it a stature which was not achieved by chance
and is nothing short of masterly. This was the last of Liebermann's pictures
to have thematic content; he now shed that content too and became
purely an impressionist, which was the logical consequence of the whole
course of his development. He painted only for the sake of the beauty
of colour, usually landscapes in bright sunlight. His confidence was
extraordinary. The rapid movements of tennis players on a sunny court,
riders in the summery atmosphere of a beach by the sea, a game of polo
with mounted riders chasing a ball, are all caught at the moment of
greatest excitement, and so too is the peaceful glow of sunlight above
houses and gardens.

Liebermann's development as a graphic artist followed a parallel course.
His first etchings were in harsh lines, showing people at work. The etching

of the weaver seated against the light among dark uprights is his most characteristic, worked out as if it were a mechanical drawing. Then, in the 1890s, the etched lines become looser, lighter, needing no detail now to show a shape in the light, able to capture movement in line as the painter could capture it in colour.

Liebermann took the path to impressionism in the sixth decade of his life, which followed such a logical course that every new step followed on naturally from its predecessor. He has been criticized, as a Jew, for being influenced by France, which is far from the case. He is not an impressionist in the French sense at all, but a hard-working artist who has never improvised. Each of his works follow on from what went before, and like Menzel he has made a wealth of sketches for every figure in a picture, always eventually choosing the most perfect form from his many studies. Liebermann has a very clear mind, the clearest of all among German painters of his generation.

Liebermann led the way in working out artistic problems, as he led impressionist ventures in general. He founded the Berlin Sezession group, waging war on behalf art and against worthless traditionalism, and the fact that he held the post of President of the Academy of the Arts in Germany for many years was evidence of the triumph of his clarity of mind.

Since those days impressionism has been recognized as a valid artistic entity, and it is now the accepted form of naturalistic vision; no longer controversial, its once revolutionary manner is almost the standard form of fine painting. In the nature of things, the number of Jewish artists painting in the impressionist style is very large. I will mention only Eugen Spiro, Joseph Oppenheimer, Ernst Oppler (recently deceased) and Frau Charlotte Behrend-Corinth, and of the younger generation the Lübeck landscape painter Erich Brill, but in fact there are far more. This is the point where the Jewish artist entered the style of his time and its products. The same path – from historical art to the modern style – has been taken in sculpture, from Marc Antokolski to Isenstein and Benno Elkan, who has created some very architectonic monuments. The assured eye of impressionism, the sharp observation it demands, which makes it the way to record things today, is behind a new form of art in black and white: the newspaper drawing. It is possible that the episodic nature of this art, the concentration on every moment, is particularly close to us today. A remarkably large number of Jews work in this area of graphic art as well as its critical counterpart, the caricature. Thomas Theodor Heine was one of the first to realize that a joke in drawing, like a joke in writing, is a sharp-edged weapon. The way in which he used it, always campaigning for some progressive idea and never just for the sake of the jokes, was classic in its way. So was his style, clear and concise in a manner that said everything necessary, could be malicious and grotesque, but was always artistic and always of formal worth. Now that this kind of art is accepted, I may mention names such as those of Trier, the wittiest of the press artists, Godal, Kroll, and Edmund Edel, each of which has his own very personal manner – for one cannot overlook an artistic genre demanding so much talent and hard work just because we still tend to believe that the value of a work of art can be judged only if it raises eternal questions. It can also be judged by the talent brought to it. Every period demands something different of its artists, since every period has a different style and lives at a different tempo.

Lesser Ury occupies a unique position in modern painting as a whole, and not just modern Jewish painting. Born in Birnbaum in 1861, and therefore fifteen years younger than Liebermann, he had his artistic training in Paris and Holland when impressionism had matured and become accepted. He quickly passed over the early stages and made his début with some brilliant landscapes. However, he had no inclination for the idyllic or wish to cast about for subjects: he fell in love with the city remarkably early and remained faithful to it. It revealed a new poetry of light and colour to him. His, however, is a very individual and personal art. Only a few very strong optical experiences have appealed to him, but they have done so lastingly. He discovered Berlin as a subject at the end of the 1880s (fig. 163); to him it is a city of coffee-houses, with glances taken in through their windows past seated customers, a city of wet streets by night with rows of lights reflected in them – a curious, gleaming, rather disturbing firework display. In the 1890s he painted in Thuringia,

FIG. 163 Lesser Ury, *The Potsdamer Platz.*

FIG. 164 Lesser Ury, *Paris.*

FIG. 165 Lesser Ury, *Praying Jew.*

in Italy and by Lake Garda, and discovered pastel as a technique for using brilliant colour with a softness that remains unreal and very poetic. Ury's art is not just naturalism, not the painting of what he sees before him, but a heightening of colour to a new beauty. His latest discoveries are Paris (fig. 164) and London. He sees their atmospheres as a contrast between spring-like radiance and foggy mists – as these cities are for anyone experiencing them with intellectual force. Unconsciously, townscapes in

Lesser Ury's work become visionary cities. Mystical experience is a very strong element in his painting.

For he is also someone else and apparently quite different: Lesser Ury the Jew, the artist who has painted the Jews in Babylon (fig. 165), poor people on a wooden bench, hands tightly clasped, staring into space, desperate people, the strongest possible contrast to Bendemann's unreal lament, Jeremiah prostrate in meditation beneath the eternal starry sky, and the gigantic figure of Moses viewing the Promised Land from afar (fig. 3). All these pictures convey an idea of Israel's longing for Zion. The forms can sometimes seem emotional, unconnected with humanity in real life, but the feeling is very genuine.

In Lesser Ury, then, the modern Jew has almost acquired stature, living in his present environment, yet consciously or unconsciously longing for Zion, experiencing reality in the real world and mysticism in the soul, and seeing opposites in himself which cause him conflict, opposites from which he finds it difficult to escape, while he cannot always come to a decision.

This conflict runs like a rift through all Jewish painting of today. On the one side are the masters of contemporary style, the impressionists, on the other side those concerned with the Jewish content of their art, ever conscious in their minds of being Jewish.

Jewish artistry is not just a question of the choice of subjects. To be a Jewish artist, it is nothing like sufficient to make use of Jewish themes, although many people thought it was in the first generation of Zionism. As in all art, however, the only legitimate criterion is genuine deep feeling. Without a doubt, what were problems of economy or politics to practical people were bound to become mysticism in art. Indeed, Jewish art could become what it was only by being mystical. Mysticism set the artist apart from the realistic art surrounding him, encouraging spiritualized, spiritual, pulsating forms glowing to the point of ecstasy.

This movement begins, to outward appearances rather hesitantly but in fact with great determination, with a generation in which the leading figures were Hermann Struck (fig. 166), Hirszenberg, and Ephraim Moses Lilien (figs 167, 168). Some quiet etchings by Wolfsfeld must be mentioned

FIG. 166   Hermann Struck,
Habdalah (etching).

FIG. 167   E.M. Lilien,
Galician Jews.

too, and here the difference between the Jews of the east and those who had settled in the west is already perceptible. The mind of the eastern Jew is more strongly permeated by mysticism, more fervent. Hirszenberg's *Goluss* [exile] is probably the most important witness anywhere to the Jewish nature of Jewish art, or at any rate the most monumental (fig. 1). The throng of exiles stepping out, spreading, becoming a great mass is an amazing sight, but its mood remains griefstricken and unconfident. Lilien does not look back very often. He prefers to look to an awareness of the present. He is a graphic artist, with spiritual meaning behind his style, which he developed from the black and white of English woodcuts, not without the influence of the coloured Japanese woodcut. Without being the greatest of artists, he none the less set the tone for the first works of art produced in Palestine itself. Even then, Jewish art was primarily graphic, and there were surely reasons for this. It is not just that much of Lilien's work is of the ephemeral character of a pamphlet –

FIG. 168 E.M. Lilien, Leaflet for the Fifth Zionist Congress in Basle.

after all, he has also illustrated the Bible, and poetry, and could equally well have painted pictures, but that did not interest him. Instead, he displays a genuine characteristic of the Jewishness of Jewish art, inclined as it is towards book illustration and graphic art because it likes ideas. Such was the case in the Middle Ages, and it is still the same today. Budko, Steinhardt and Rahel Szalit are also illustrators.

The essence of this attitude is that it leads further and further away from reality. Arising entirely from feeling, from an ardent sense of being linked to the soul of Israel, it is in the strongest possible contrast to impressionism, which was all to do with the eye. What it depicts becomes expression to the point of ecstasy. Paradoxical and apparently superficial as this may sound, it is a fact that impressionism is the art of the assimilated, while Jewish art lives consciously in expressionism, and for very deep reasons. Here I am not of course speaking of expressionists who, like Rudolf Lévy or Moïse Kisling in Paris, seek strong expression in naturalistic subjects and are really still painting in the impressionistic,

255

FIG. 169 Jakob Steinhardt, *The Widow.*

FIG. 170 Ludwig Meidner, *Self-Portrait* (etching).

western tradition, but of those who have given expressionism a form of
its own, and a very Jewish one, perhaps the real seeds of a Jewish style.

The important names in Germany are those of Jakob Steinhardt (b.
1887 in Zerkow, Posen) and Ludwig Meidner (b. 1884 in Bornstadt in
Silesia). Steinhardt's graphic art does not set out from anatomical form at
all, but from expression (fig. 169). He experiences gestures and body
movement as an ecstasy of pain and piety. Expression is felt to the very
fingertips in their strongly arching, stretched, curving lines. His people
seem almost fleshless. Meidner's themes are seldom explicitly Jewish, but
his mind and ecstatic manner are (fig. 170). His writings – he has written
autobiographical material – are like fragments of artistic ideas. He falls

passionately on people and things and wrenches expression from them with extraordinary violence. His works might have been created in a fever. Extraordinary turns, foreshortenings and bends, almost impossible anatomically, seem to come from the sphere of prophecy, even in portraits. He likes to situate himself high above his subject, at the intellectual centre of the picture, as if meditating on it.

The many artists who come straight from areas further east and have retained the eastern spirit are quite different in character. Their mystical foundations go even deeper; the picture is less of an act, more of a quiet vision on a large scale. The most forceful of these artists is Marc Chagall (born in Vitebsk in 1890). His picture are extremely colourful, but not with the colour of light shed down on the world: it is the rustic colour of carved rustic crafts (fig. 171). His mind inhabits a primitive world which is painted in glaring colours, with hard, carved outlines. He is at home among colourful houses in colourful villages and with the quiet people who live in them, and his pictures always express a longing for liberation from the narrow sphere that he loves although it oppresses him. Jankel Adler, a very individual, analytical artist now working in Düsseldorf, and Lasar Segall, born in Vilna in 1889, are from the same emotional background. Segall's development is by way of Paris through Cubism, whose primitive structures are congenial to his own manner. Following these, a great throng of younger artists are emerging, some of them very gifted, for instance Barczynski. However, it is still too early to pick out the masters of the future from among them.

And so the art of the Jewish east finds its way back to the west from which it once set out. An admirable faith has kept the old ideas alive in human minds over the centuries, despite outward subjection to Slav domains. Just as the Yiddish language is really a kind of mediaeval German, so the same notes struck in the pictures of the German Haggadah manuscripts of around 1500 echo on in the works of eastern Jewish painters. There is the same primitive strength of expression, the same way of confining oneself to essentials, the same mystic power of those who are inwardly oppressed and find release in pictures. This art is mystic art. Emotions echo within it, emotions still so pure and involuntary that

FIG. 171 Marc Chagall, *The Rabbi.*

they pass on only what they directly share.

Jewish art today stands at the parting of the ways, like Judaism itself. While many of its great talents are turning to mainstream European art and becoming almost entirely assimilated, others are seeking the way towards an art of their own. Jewish impressionists and Jewish expressionists oppose one another like rationalism and mysticism. These two contrasting views have defined themselves with extraordinary clarity in their struggle to win esteem in the world.

In the last resort, however, they are only relative. There can be no total assimilation even for one who strives for it, no complete submerging of the artist's identity into the local style. Art does not depend on the will. Instinct creates art, the compulsion of a creative soul, and consequently there is a Jewish element in every work of art by a Jew, even if he denies it. The whole course of the history of Jewish art proves the point. In short: to outward appearances, Jewish art is dependent on the art of the countries in which it is created. But it has other experiences, and experiences them in other ways, so that we find very distinct Jewish variants of art everywhere.

Naturally they are more marked the more conscious of itself the Jewish life of the time is, and the greater the artist's own sense of being Jewish. Consequently, they are most obvious in periods such as the end of classical antiquity, the Gothic Middle Ages, the eastern Jewish Baroque period, and in the strongly confessional and consciously Jewish youth of the present day. Hence the constructive power of those artists who come from the east and are still deeply rooted in a Judaic spirit.

Jewish art is always the art of the soul. Since the beginning of its history, Israel has striven for profundity. Its intellectual life was a religious life, and hence, even at quite an early period, its strong feeling for the moral structure of state and community and its love of social justice. It is always aspiring, seeking the solution of earthly things in eternity. Mysticism is the characteristic feature of its life and art, and to Israel, mysticism means the elevation of earthly existence to eternity. Mysticism is the Sabbath among the days of the week.

Our time as a whole, however, has its sights set on achievement. The intellect rather than the emotions provides its artistic tasks. They are solved through forms of art that are part of worldly life. The leading stylistic influences are slowly but inexorably becoming those of architects and engineers. However, a realistic look at problems does not exclude creativity. On the contrary – nothing is a well-formed work that is not shaped by the creative mind. Because we assert Judaism, Jewish art exists. That is as true of its practical as of its pictorial tasks. The industrial complexes being built in Palestine, the settlements of Jewish farmers in the south of Russia, the synagogue buildings in many places designed not just for divine worship but as spiritual assembly points in the life of the community, are functional buildings in which spiritual and objective demands unite. They point the way leading on from the present, from the captive Jewish spirit of the ghettos into the free spirit of the future.

AFTERWORD

to the 1929 edition

I T IS impossible to mention all the sources upon which I have drawn
in the long process of preparing to write this book. A history of
Jewish art demands laborious and very intensive work. There are very
few real works of research on its monuments. Finds have mostly come to
light by chance during excavations and archaeological investigations, and
accounts of them are published in obscure journals or only when occasion offers. Very frequently their Jewish character is recognized only after
many years, as was the case, for instance, with the synagogue of Elche.
The existence of Jewish monuments from all periods and all countries is
thus itself very indicative of the history of Jewish art as a whole, and
indeed the fact that they are found in the most remote places is a pre-
requisite of their study. The most important works I have used, particularly for the illustrations, follow below: they usually indicate further sources
of information.

R.A. Stewart Macalister, *Excavations in Gezer*, London 1912 (fig. 7). E.
Seelin and C. Watzinger, *Jericho*, Leipzig 1913 (figs 8, 24, 25). G. Schumacher
and C. Steuernagel, *Tell el Mutesellim*, Leipzig 1908 (figs 9, 10, 11, 22, 23,
26, 27, 28, 29, 31). E. Sellin, *Tell Ta'anak*, Vienna 1904 (figs 12, 32). Palestine Exploration Fund, *Annuals* (figs 13, 14, 15, 41). Melchior de Vogué, *Le
temple de Jerusalem*, Paris 1864/65 (figs 16, 37). Bliss and Macalister, *Excavations in Palestine*, London 1902 (fig. 33). *Publications of the Princeton University Expedition to Syria 1904/5* (figs 35, 36). Kahl and Watzinger, *Die
Synagogen in Galiläa*, Berlin 1916 (figs 43, 44, 45, 46, 49, 50, 51, 52, 53).
Garucci, *Storia dell'arte christiana*, Prato 1880/81 (fig. 81). Peters and
Thiersch, *Painted Tombs*, London 1905 (fig. 57). Becker, *Malta Sotteranea*
(figs 62, 63). Wiegand and Schrade, *Priene*, Berlin 1904 (fig. 69). *Révue*

Archéologique 1884 (figs 71, 72, 73). *Notizie degli scavi* Vol. 20 (fig. 83). N. Müller, *Katakombe am Monteverde*, Leipzig 1913 (fig. 84). Stassoff and Gunzburg, *L'ornement hébreu*, Berlin 1905 (figs 91, 92, 93, 94, 95, 96). Müller and Scholosser, *Die Haggadah von Serajevo*, Vienna 1898 (figs 97–107, 120, 121, 122, 135–141). D. Henriques de Castro, *Auswahl von Grabsteinen*, Leiden 1883 (figs 143, 144, 145).

The principal journals and periodical publications consulted have been: The Bulletin of the Society for the Maintenance of Jewish Artistic Monuments, Menorah and Rimon. Photographs from the Kaiser Friedrich Museum of Berlin, the Luitpold Museum of Würzburg, the art collection of the Jewish Community of Berlin, the photographic publishing firms of Dr. Stödtner in Berlin, and of Füller in Worms.

I owe special thanks for the provision of particularly rare photographs to Professor D. Lietzemann and Dr. Volbach, curator of the Kaiser Friedrich Museum.

ERNST COHN-WIENER
Berlin,
December 1929

AFTERWORD
to the 1995 German edition

THE AUTHOR of this book was an art historian of wide-ranging interests and knowledge.

Born in 1882 in Tilsit, Ernst Cohn-Wiener studied art history, archaeology and philosophy in Berlin and Heidelberg. Among his earliest works, published as early as 1910, is a book on the history of the development of style. While principally active as a university lecturer in Berlin, Cohn-Wiener went on a journey of research to Russia and the Near East in 1924–25. His interest in the art of Asia was reflected in his study *Asia. Einführung in die Kunstwelt des Ostens* ['Asia. An introduction to the artistic world of the east'], which appeared in 1929, as did his *Jüdische Kunst.* These two books are regarded as his main works.

In 1934 he fled the National Socialist régime, going to Baroda in India, where he continued to pursue his career as an art historian. He left India, obviously for reasons of health, and found a new refuge in New York, where he died in 1941.

This brief sketch in itself shows that Cohn-Wiener was not one of those scholars who specialize in a small section of the European history of art. Rather, he devoted his mind to a very broad field reaching geographically from Europe to Asia, and historically ranging from the modern period back to antiquity, a fact that also explains his study of archaeology.

This broad intellectual horizon and depth of thought in the treatment of individual objects determine the tone of the present book, *JEWISH ART*: *Its History from the Beginnings to the Present Day* (Berlin, 1929), the first comprehensive survey of the manifestations of Jewish art from antiquity to the twentieth century.

The year of publication, 1929, is surprising in view of the findings and previous work on the subject then at the author's disposal, for in 1929 the study of Jewish art was still a very young discipline; research on various areas of it had been done, to very different degrees, while light was not shed on other areas until later.

None the less – and although of course Cohn-Wiener could not know of new discoveries and articles written after 1929, so that he could not include them in his study – this book is still up to date and by no means a fossil. Why? To answer that question we must look at it from two points of view, each of them referring back to history. One concerns the year 1929 and the state of research in the preceding period upon which Cohn-Wiener could call. The other looks back from today, the year 1995, at continued research over the past sixty-six years, which was interrupted in this area (of all others) during the period of Nazi rule and the Second World War, but in which great progress has been made since around 1950. Here we have to take into account the discovery of new finds, the publication of individual studies, general surveys, etc. Consequently the question of how far these more recent studies contradict Cohn-Wiener's ideas, and how we are to assess his book of 1929 today, is an important one.

The state of research until 1929 presents an irregular and yet a consistent picture, for the most important areas in the field had already been tackled, if not in satisfactory depth.

If we leave aside the various phases of the building of the temple in Jerusalem, study of which (after the somewhat fantastic ideas of the Middle Ages) really begins in the sixteenth century, relying on the Biblical accounts as valid written sources in a manner comparable to the methods of those classical archaeologists who sought to explore the sites and structure of the buildings of antiquity with their classical texts ready to hand, then the study of Jewish art really begins in the second half of the nineteenth century. At that time English and French scholars in particular began exploring the geographical area of Palestine, including the ruins of the synagogues of antiquity, which were only correctly identified as such quite late in the day. There were synagogues of the early type in Galilee, in the north of Israel, described by Kohl and Watzinger in their standard work of 1916. Cohn-Wiener was able to make use of their work. Only a little was known about synagogue building in late antiquity, with its mosaic floors. The synagogue of Beth Alpha was discovered in 1929, the year when this book came out (E.L. Sukenik's account was published in 1932), yet Cohn-Wiener already cites the find.

Ancient synagogues from earlier excavations, in countries outside Palestine, were known as sporadic finds, for instance the synagogues of Hammam-Lif in Tunisia and Priene in Turkey. However, comprehensive works on all periods of synagogue architecture in antiquity and in all the major countries of its occurrence did not appear until after 1929, beginning with E.L. Sukenik's *Ancient Synagogues in Palestine and Greece*, London 1934. All other works on the subject appeared after the Second World War.

Particularly important for research, from our present point of view, was the discovery in the 1930s of the synagogue in Dura Europos. This, the only such building of antiquity with an extensive cycle of frescos, overturned all previous ideas about the ban on pictorial decoration, and was not known to Cohn-Wiener.

The first studies of ancient funerary art were also made in the nineteenth century, in Palestine, in the Jewish catacombs of Rome and later on in Malta. However, the large catacomb complexes of Beth Shearim, so important for research, were not excavated until the thirties and after; accounts were published by B. Mazar in 1935–40 and N. Avigad in 1953–58.

The Jewish art of the Middle Ages consists chiefly of two areas, book illumination and synagogue architecture, while illustrations in printed books and a considerable amount of works of craft in textiles and metals are preserved only from a post-mediaeval period, and were made at that time.

1898 saw the first publication of a facsimile edition of a painted Hebrew manuscript. This was the Sarajevo Haggadah (14th-century Spain), edited by D.H. Müller and J. von Schlosser, with a remarkable appendix 'Zur Geschichte der jüdischen Handschriften' ['On the History of the Jewish Manuscripts'] by David Kaufmann, who also wrote various other articles on related subjects. The first comprehensive work on the subject appeared in 1909 and was by Heinrich Frauberger (*Verzierte hebräische Schrift und jüdischer Buchschmuck*, ['Decorated Hebrew script and Jewish book ornamentation'], Frankfurt am Main 1909). Frauberger arranges the manuscripts by type (scrolls, books, single leaves) and analyses their artistic design. The next manuscript was not published in its entirety as a facsimile until 1927. This was the Darmstadt Haggadah (Germany, 15th century). The editors were Bruno Italiener and Aron Freimann, who continued to study and publish works on the subject of illuminated books until the twenties.

Around the turn of the century, however, the scholars who devoted themselves to the areas of book illumination, synagogues and craftsmanship were David Kaufmann and Heinrich Frauberger in particular.

A 'Society for the Study of Jewish Artistic Monuments' was founded in Frankfurt am Main; Frauberger sets out its aim and purposes in a book of 1900. He was also responsible for the first published findings on synagogue architecture (*Über Bau und Ausschmuckung alter Synagogen* ['On the Building and Ornamentation of Ancient Synagogues'], Frankfurt am Main 1901), while Kaufmann devoted himself in his essays to individual buildings, among them the two medieval synagogues of Toledo (1899). The first general works on synagogue architecture were by Alfred Grotte, who published his *Deutsche, böhmische und polnische Synagogentypen vom XI. bis Anfang des XIX. Jahrhunderts* ['German, Bohemian and Polish Types of Synagogues from the 11th to the Beginning of the 19th Century'] in Berlin in 1915, and after 1916 published material on the Polish synagogues as well. He also wrote many of the articles on architecture in the *Jüdisches Lexikon* (5 vols, 1927–30). Another study is by Richard Krautheimer in his *Mittelalterliche Synagogen* ['Mediaeval Synagogues'], Berlin 1927, which is chiefly concerned with the mediaeval synagogues of Germany. On the other hand, the European synagogues after the sixteenth century, particularly those of Poland and Italy, were known only partially at this time, from Grotte's work of 1915, already cited, and from later articles on individual subjects; the book by A. Breier, M. Eisler and M. Grunwald on *Holzsynagogen in Polen* ['Wooden Synagogues in Poland'] did not appear until 1934.

Research into Jewish craftsmanship also began around 1900, with a work by Frauberger (*Über alte Kultusgegenstände in Synagoge und Haus* ['On Old Cultic Items in Synagogue and Home'], Frankfurt am Main 1903). Aron Freimann, already mentioned in connection with books and art, also published essays on works of craftsmanship until the twenties; such items, with a few exceptions, survive from the sixteenth century and later.

The situation before 1929, when Ernst Cohn-Wiener wrote his book, is a scene of scholarly activity in a relatively young branch of art history, one in which many separate themes have already been dealt with, but with general surveys of distinct periods and artistic genres in different countries still very rare. So the brevity of the bibliography at the end of the book is not surprising. Cohn-Wiener mentions only a few complete books, but has drawn on a number of essays.

We thus get a picture of a situation in scholarship basically comprising isolated studies of individual objects, a situation which is only just beginning to approach wider research.

In this context Cohn-Wiener ventures on a work dealing with material over a period of three millennia. For the first time he brings together the findings of his time, disproportionate as they were, to provide a general survey. As his contents pages show, he avoids listing the material itself. After an introduction, he divides the book into five chapters, dispensing with subheadings and other subdivisions as we know them today. The division follows broad historical viewpoints; he puts the whole period from the Middle Ages until the eighteenth century together in a section which he calls '*Goluss* and Ghetto', i.e., he sees the Jewish Middle Ages as lasting until the Enlightenment, and he dispenses with any more detailed subdivision of it.

Cohn-Wiener does not take the historian's usual path, but instead places the material in the context of his own thoughts and ideas on basic questions such as the attitude of the people of Israel to art in general and pictorial art in particular, and their relationship with neighbouring peoples. He shows art against the background of external conditions changing with the course of time. He succeeds in grasping the essence of Jewish art, and that essence does not change; only its outward appearance is subject to modification at certain times, and while the more recent findings discovered since the publication of this book may provide more detailed information, they hardly disturb the picture Cohn-Wiener provides of the nature of Jewish art. The power of the book perhaps lies in this, and in its ability to make a useful statement in our own time.

However, let us go into detail.

Cohn-Wiener gives his *Introduction* the subtitle 'The Basic Question'. This basic question concerns the definition of Jewish art, its existence despite the prohibition on pictorial representation, and its style. He distinguishes between the ideas of God held by the people of Israel and those of their environment, pointing up the difference by the example of classical Greece, which he sees as a sensuous nation regarding its highest attainment as the beautiful depiction of a god. Israel, on the other hand, had 'come to believe in something transcendental, not bound to the structures of the visible world'. That belief 'led to the acknowledgement of one God, a wholly spiritual and immaterial being, who was therefore impossible either to imagine or to depict'.

That is to say, the ban on pictorial art applies to the divine, to any representation of God, and is carried over to what is near God. 'No free-standing sculpture and no figurative images on holy things were tolerated in Israel.'

However there was and is Jewish art, since a wish to express things in structural form existed. 'The absence of pictorial images does not mean an absence of structural form.' In order to provide that form, Israel fell back on the style of its geographical area and its period. Cohn-Wiener writes, with good reason, that Jewish art depended on the style of its environment, and consequently in this sense 'it has no absolute independence'. Interestingly, he comments that in his own time excessive emphasis was also placed on form and style, which could lead to a negative assessment of Jewish art – that at least has hardly changed today.

Israel, he writes, was first and foremost a thinking people, not a creative one, and in this context he points out the great quantity of literary production. Finally, however, the people did produce art, but to a Jew form was only the means, 'not an end in itself'. Jewish artistic expression paid less attention to outward form and far more to content, the internal and spiritual element.

In his first chapter, 'The Land that Israel Conquered', he deals with the early period when the kingdom was coming into being. He describes the Israelites of the time as a nomadic people owning portable goods but having no architecture when they conquered Canaan. Canaan itself, he says, was no shrine of high culture, for 'it had always been the subject of dispute or a battleground for its neighbours, never a breeding ground for culture'.

The breadth of the author's knowledge, which is not limited to the field of Jewish art, is shown in the account of those neighbours and their cultures. He grasps their essence briefly and illuminatingly, particularly the cultures of the Egyptians, Hittites and Phoenicians, who all left their mark on the land of Canaan in different ways. He describes Canaan itself and its cities (particularly Jericho) as a culture marked by different influences, and one with which Israel now came into contact.

The chapter on 'The Time of the Kings' follows. While the author sees David, the conqueror of Jerusalem, as a clever politician and leader of the people, he presents the figure of Solomon as the first to be part of a royal culture. Solomon's 'temple and his palace, important in both their design and their decoration, were the nation's greatest cultural expression, and they remained so for a long period'. Solomon sought models for his buildings among the Phoenicians, says Cohn-Wiener, a view still held today, and indeed confirmed by the Bible.

Cohn-Wiener also describes the various techniques in use at the time. He distinguishes between the technical abilities of the Israelites, who like the Phoenicians were able to cover objects with thin gold leaf (this passage particularly concerns the interior decoration of the temple), and the technique of metal-founding, still unknown to the Israelites at the time. These tasks had to be carried out by craftsmen from Tyre.

He points up connections with the culture of Israel's neighbours, particularly the Phoenicians, and recognizes the discrepancy between the theoretical absence of pictures in a building related to religious observance like the temple, and its pictorial ornamentation in practice with cherubs, etc., which he explains as deriving from the culture of the environment, from which, however, the Israelites clearly set themselves apart by the absence of an image of God.

The author is very enlightening in his attempt to explain the buildings on the temple mount and other large buildings elsewhere, some of them of later date, their furnishings and the small craft objects found in them, as well as the early funerary complexes, in terms of the art and techniques encountered by the Israelites. At the same time he describes the manner in which the previously nomadic people developed a popular art of their own in the course of time.

The chapter on 'Israel Among the Peoples of Antiquity' begins with the destruction of Solomon's temple in the year 586 BCE. He explains very cogently how Israel, geographically placed among the other peoples of the Near East, was also exposed to their heathen cultural ideas, against which it had to defend and assert itself in order to be able to rebuild the temple at the end of the sixth century. Its holy of holies remained empty, for the ark of the covenant had been looted. This building was not an example of splendour and magnificence; its point was that it was a temple.

There was a political equivalent to Israel's spiritual confrontation with the various peoples of the region. 'After Israel's return to its own country it would have been possible for a Jewish culture to come into being. The beginnings of such a thing were present and beginning to develop. However, the land did not have peace, for its overlords kept changing over the next few centuries ... '

After the Persians, Alexander the Great, the Ptolemies of Egypt and the Syrian rulers the country did not regain anything like a government and culture of its own until the time of the Maccabees (the second century BCE).

However, this period also saw 'the infiltration of Greek art into the east', and for the Jews it meant confrontation with Hellas and the Orient. In this tense situation impressive works of art were in fact created; the palatial complexes were secular architecture, but there were also some works of art relating to genuinely Jewish elements, to the rule of the Maccabees and their coinage, the first to bear Jewish symbols, and in the religious area to the renovation of the temple under Herod and the first funerary complexes, such as those in the valley of Kidron near Jerusalem, or the graves of the kings (the first century CE). Structurally, both the temple and the graves adopt elements of classical architecture in their architectonic design, but in themselves the complexes of buildings follow deeply Jewish lines.

As before, Cohn-Wiener's dual approach is evident in this chapter: he explains individual objects in terms of art history, but situates them in the context of cultural history, dealing not only with those works of art that had religious connections but also with secular architecture, which reached great heights, in particular under Herod and in Samaria.

From the time after the destruction of the temple (70 CE) and the failure of the Bar Kochba uprising (132–135 CE) he picks out, in particular, the early synagogues in the north of Palestine, and begins to look at the art of the Diaspora. His account of the early Galilean synagogues, built from about 200 CE, is thorough and circumspect, but in our present state of knowledge we can see that some small errors have crept in. For instance, he suggests that the synagogue at Capernaum (Kfar Nahum) was the only one to have had courtyard architecture; today we know that the same layout occurred in other synagogues. These small lacunae can be overlooked, but in discussing the synagogues of late antiquity and their mosaic floors he comes up against the barrier of the limited knowledge of his time. In fact the building in Beth Alpha had only just been discovered, and he does mention its mosaic floors, but hardly comments on them at all, which is understandable. Only after 1929 was there a new debate which overturned the old idea that abstention from pictorial depiction was obligatory, something that became really clear only from the synagogue of Dura-Europos, which was not discovered until 1932, and which, with its lavish cycles of frescos, gives us a different idea of the ornamentation of synagogues. The idea of the ban on images is now rejected, but the whole debate occurred only after the publication of Cohn-Wiener's book. Something not affected by more recent discoveries, however, is his account of the absence of any depiction of God. The figurative scenes on the mosaic floors and frescos illustrate Jewish religious ideas of the time, but unlike heathen and Christian works of art do not invite the paying of devotions to the figures themselves.

His account of Jewish symbolism in small works of craftsmanship is very progressive, and the same is true of his the interpretation of the mosaic floor of the synagogue in Hammam-Lif in Tunisia, which he already recognizes as a symbolic representation of Paradise, even though the first comprehensive work on Jewish symbolism did not appear until 1935 (Rachel Wischnitzer-Bernstein, *Gestalten und Symbole der jüdische Kunst* ['Figures and Symbols in Jewish Art'], Berlin 1935). His interpretation of the symbolism in the Roman catacombs, their sarcophagi, and the gold glasses found there is also illuminating.

Cohn-Wiener devotes a great deal of room to symbolism, for this is where the religious Jewish content obviously lies, removed from the formal element, and to the 'change of emphasis from service in the temple to veneration of the Torah'. He shows how a development from the first isolated motifs to a rich symbolic vocabulary uniting several motifs and themes into a single 'picture' could occur. 1929 was an early date for him to recognize this development, and opinions on it have not changed to this day.

The following chapter, '*Goluss* and Ghetto', covers the period from the Middle Ages to the eighteenth century without any further historical subdivisions, since external conditions for the Jews of Europe remained the same. The pre-requisite for the free development of the arts was absent in the *galut* or *goluss,* i.e. freedom and the right to creativity and personal development, and moreover the free development of a public which can lead to a work of art's becoming an experience. Life in the ghetto made that public a very limited one. 'Dispersal among other nations became enslavement by them in the Middle Ages.'

However, Cohn-Wiener draws distinctions. He recognizes that the early encounter with Islam was a fruitful one, for 'there was no inner opposition between Muslims and Jews'. He deals very extensively with the synagogues of Spain built under the influence of Islamic art, and with book illumination from the Islamic countries, very fine in their artwork at first, becoming coarser later.

He uses the Spanish Haggadah manuscripts, stylistically influenced by Christian art of the Gothic period, as an opportunity to look at the situation in the Christian world, and goes very extensively into the painting of these manuscripts, explaining the Jewish content of the pictures in contrast to the Gothic, Christian form.

Cohn-Wiener sees the inheritance of Spanish Judaism in art after the expulsion of the Jews from Spain in 1492 as very clearly passing to Italy. 'Only Italy developed a Jewish culture of similar importance', since the Italy of the Renaissance, with its liberal ideas, offered the right conditions for cultural development. He discusses at length book illumination of the Renaissance period and synagogue architecture from the sixteenth century onwards, particularly in Padua and Venice, and describes the items of furnishing which have been preserved. His penetrating study of these fields is surprising in that when he wrote individual items had certainly been described in articles and were known from them, but there were no general surveys, so that Cohn-Wiener was obliged to take the first overall view of the items then known.

The synagogue architecture of mediaeval Germany was a different case, since it had been comprehensively covered by Krautheimer in 1927.

Cohn-Wiener proceeds country by country, his account of synagogues in Spain and Italy being followed by those of Germany and eastern Europe. He deals with the synagogues of Worms and Regensburg, Prague and Kazimierz in Cracow, describing the field of tension between the contemporary architectural style of the Christian environment and the Jewish spatial structuring required for an area to be used as a synagogue.

This opposition between fixed outward forms and Jewish content is also clear in his discussion of Ashkenazi book illumination. Here again, as in classical antiquity and late antiquity, he finds symbolism very important, since it is used to express what is specifically Jewish. On the other hand, his account of Jewish art in the Netherlands is very brief. He gives a short description of the seventeenth-century Portuguese synagogue in Amsterdam, and a rather longer one of the seventeenth-century Sephardi cemeteries in Ouderkerk, which bear Biblical scenes in defiance of the usual custom. He explains these figurative scenes as early assimilation of the former Spanish Jews into their Dutch environment, a precursor of the situation which would develop in England and during the Enlightenment in Germany. Today, however, we would differ from him, for the Sephardi Jews who went to Holland or Altona at the end of the sixteenth century had lived as forcible converts for a period of eighty to a hundred years and were familiar with Christian usages, which they had initially imported into their own art, although by now they had officially returned to Judaism. We have evidence in the fact that there are no such figurative scenes in the nineteenth century, the most important period of emancipation and assimilation. However, the necessary pre-requisites for such conclusions to be drawn were not available around 1929.

Cohn-Wiener sees the Ashkenazi world of Central and Eastern Europe as quite unlike that of the confident Spanish Jews with their coats of arms and international trade relations. 'The Middle Ages were not over for the Ashkenazi Jews.'

Cohn-Wiener regards the Jewish art of Poland and the wooden synagogues of the seventeenth and eighteenth centuries as 'rustic' for lack of artistic stimulus, i.e. as a kind of folk art, with paintings and rich symbolism which does not rise into the realms of culture, a view still held today.

The final chapter, 'The Way to the Present Day', traces the path of the Jewish artist leaving the ghetto, training in academies of art, and stepping forward at last as an individual. In the process Cohn-Wiener condemns the architects of the nineteenth-century synagogue buildings who followed the many styles of historicism and failed to express any emancipatory ideas. A change, he says, came in the twentieth century with Erich Mendelsohn. It was otherwise with painters. Cohn-Wiener describes Eduard Bendemann as the first painter to devote himself to Biblical subjects in the field of historical painting, and Moritz Oppenheim as the first to bring the Jewish world into genre paintings. He traces a line from Joseph Israels to Max Liebermann and Lesser Ury. However, he considers that only the group of artists including Hermann Struck, Samuel Hirszenberg and E.M. Lilien achieved something new that could really be described as Jewish painting and graphic art, and in this context he alludes to the founding of the Bezalel School in Jerusalem in the year 1906. His assessment of these artists is still very up to date. He concludes: 'They point the way leading on from the present, from the captive Jewish spirit of the ghettos into the free spirit of the future.' This was reasonable enough in a survey of 1929, but the immediate future was to interrupt the development he foresees abruptly. On the other hand, we can see now that those early twentieth-century artists who emigrated to Palestine at the time were to lay the foundations of painting in the new state of Israel.

Study of questions of detail has shown that some of Cohn-Wiener's ideas must be revised today, but that the overall picture he gives, covering a period of more than three thousand years, is still relevant. The value of his book lies here, and not least in his vigorous and precise use of language, his setting of Jewish art against the cultural history of the peoples of the Near East and Europe. The courage to undertake such a survey as early as 1929 led to an enduring success.

HANNELORE KÜNZL
Heidelberg,
June 1995